ALEXANDER MARSHALL

EVANGELIST, AUTHOR & PIONEER

Alexander Marshall

ALEXANDER MARSHALL

EVANGELIST, AUTHOR & PIONEER

by

JOHN HAWTHORN

1988
Published by
GOSPEL TRACT PUBLICATIONS
411 Hillington Road, Glasgow G52 4BL, Scotland

ISBN 0 948417 33 1

Typeset, printed and bound by
GOSPEL TRACT PUBLICATIONS
411 Hillington Road, Glasgow G52 4BL, Scotland

Foreword

A.M. have been the well-known initials of four men of considerable repute in our day: ANDREW MILLER, London, writer and evangelist, author of *Short Papers on Church History*, etc.; ALBERT MIDLANE, Newport, I.W., poet and preacher, author of *There's a Friend for Little Children, Revive Thy Work, O Lord*, and some 200 hymns; ANDREW MURRAY, apostle of holiness of South Africa, author of many well-known books; and ALEXANDER MARSHALL, evangelist, whose initials are perhaps the best known of the four, on account of his long years of labour in many lands and the millions of times the initials were used in books, tracts, and magazines in many languages.

That Alex. Marshall was a born evangelist and one sent of God with the Message, few who ever heard him or knew him would think of denying. In my judgment, I knew of no man who so persistently kept "evangelism" as the mission of his life; and of no man who had more real converts in most parts of the world than A.M.; and many of these converts became themselves soul-winners.

Besides, no man wrote so many tracts and Gospel messages. They flowed from his pen, and dealt with matters of the moment and things which happened ages ago, yet all was used to hang the application of the three R's thereon. Certainly no man was the means of putting so many into circulation by writing, by paying for issue, by assisting others in circulation, and, by no means least, by personal distribution. His pockets were ever full of Gospel ammunition, and an opportunity was seldom missed of firing a Gospel bullet, which usually hit the mark.

The blessing which alone has followed his one tract, *GOD'S WAY OF SALVATION*, which might aptly be termed "the essence of A.M.'s preaching," was worth living a whole lifetime for.

As a preacher he was unique. We have been through several A.M. Gospel Campaigns during the last 30 years, and wondered again and again how any unsaved sinner, with any thought concerning eternal realities, could leave the meeting without the knowledge of salvation. His methods were neither spectacular, demonstrative, nor emotional; he used no undue pressure, no body-motion to gain converts; yet numbers were saved through the preaching, waited for the after meetings, found peace at home, or turned up weeks after glorifying God for His salvation.

With the learnèd, laboured, or popular discourse he had little sympathy. After hearing a preacher giving an address without making the Gospel plain, he usually remarked, "A teachifying Gospel," or, "Not as much Gospel as would save a midge!"

So firm was his conviction that "Christ died for all," that he almost seemed to relish a discussion with one leaning to Calvinistic views. One of his favourite points was, "If all those to be saved were chosen in Christ before the foundation of the world (Eph 1:4), what did Paul mean when he said of Andronicus and Junia, 'who were *in Christ before me?'* " (Rom 16:7). We never yet heard a satisfactory answer to the question; nor did we ever see those whom he opposed, part with him in anything but a friendly manner.

A.M. seemed built for travelling, and almost relished it. He would part from us on a trip to Russia, Canada, or New Zealand just as though he were going for a week-end to London. Then he would turn up three months or years after, apparently in the same dress, just as if he had come off the train from Edinburgh or some neighbouring town. Yet everywhere he sought by lip and printed page to "preach Christ."

That the life of this remarkable evangelist, collected from sources none too plentiful, will prove of real interest and stimulus to all who heard beloved A.M. during his many years of preaching, to all who have read any of his almost innumerable writings, to all who knew and loved him intimately or remotely, and to all who love true lip and life evangelism, is certain. At least it has proved a concise record of happy remembrance to one who knew and loved A.M. for many years.

HyP

Preface

In the course of his extensive travelling as an Evangelist, Mr Marshall formed a wide circle of friends in lands as widely separated as New Zealand and Alaska, or as San Francisco and Petrograd. Many of these friends were brought to the Saviour through his preaching, and not a few have expressed the hope that some memorial of his life and of the ministry by which they have been spiritually enriched should be prepared.

It was the author's privilege to enjoy the confidence and friendship of Mr. Marshall for many years, and to be associated with him in much that he did, more especially during the later period of his life, when the mellowing influences of age and experience were producing their choicest fruits. At that period the most reticent of men frequently become reminiscent; and much that is contained in this brief biography was received direct during intimate talks, some of which took place a few days before his Home-call.

For this reason it has been a peculiar pleasure, at the request of Mrs. Marshall, to gather together some of the scattered threads of an intensely busy life and to show them in relation to the remarkable work of grace in which the subject of this memoir played no inconsiderable part.

The aim throughout has been to show "what God hath wrought," and to recall the former days in order that others should follow Mr. Marshall's faith. If in the present season of testing this little volume is the means of encouraging a new generation of believers to enter into and preserve the heritage won for them by Alexander Marshall and his contemporaries, it will be labour well spent.

JOHN HAWTHORN

Contents

I	Religious Struggle and Experience	13
II	Work and Witness	24
III	Pioneering in Canada	41
IV	Fruitful and Happy Years	51
V	Defence and Confirmation of the Gospel	61
VI	Fulfilling His Ministry	70
VII	Into Regions Beyond	81
VIII	Personal Gifts	102
IX	The Pen of a Ready Writer	113
X	Mr. Marshall's Correspondence	123
XI	The Activities of a Veteran	129
XII	A Bright Eventide	140
	Places Visited by A. Marshall	150
	Friends and Colleagues of A. Marshall	152

Illustrations

Alexander Marshall	Frontispiece
Facsimile, Outline Address, A.M.	93
Facsimile of Letter from Mr. R.C. Chapman	109
Mr. Marshall in the Uniform of the Soldiers' Christian Association	125
Mr. Marshall at his favourite work	131

CHAPTER I

Religious Struggle and Experience

The picturesque town of Stranraer, situated at the head of Loch Ryan, in Wigtownshire, is the principal town in a country rich with the memories of devoted servants of Christ. Within a few miles of the town is Wigtown Bay, where Margaret Wilson and Margaret Maclauchlan, the Wigtownshire martyrs, were tied to stakes fastened in the sand at low water, and allowed to drown in the incoming tide. A short journey by road or rail takes the traveller to fair Anwoth by the Solway, known world-wide as the parish where saintly Samuel Rutherford exercised a gracious ministry. Of more recent years, Murray McNeil Caird, J.P. Struthers, John Walbran, Geo. Adams, J.M. Hamilton, and other well-known men were signally used of God during periods of revival blessing.

In this atmosphere, and a worthy successor to the Covenanters, John Wallace Marshall, during the middle portion of the last century, carried on the business of a tailor and outfitter; but like William Carey, his calling in life was to preach Christ. He carried on his business to pay expenses. He was nick-named in the town "Holy Marshall," on account of the stand he took for the Lord. A street preacher, the poor man's minister and lawyer, he conducted services in the wards of the poorhouse, in cottages, and wherever there was an open door.

13

He took a special interest in children, and if he always had a word for the grown-ups, he also had a "sweetie" ever ready for the bairns. His wife was a true helpmeet, and in her own domain and in a quiet way showed the same devotion to the Lord.

In 1841 a notable evangelical movement in Scotland caused no little stir. James Morison, the young minister of Clerk's Lane Secession Church in Kilmarnock, was dealt with by the Presbytery and forced to resign his charge. The extreme Calvinism of the period looked upon the declaration of the young preacher that Jesus died for the sins of all men without exception or distinction as a dangerous doctrine, and as such to be resisted. The result was that Morison formed the Evangelical Union, more familiarly known as "Morisonians," which at the period of which we write was the strongest evangelistic force in Scotland. Mr. Marshall was an out-and-out supporter of Dr. Morison, and his view of the teachings of Scripture regarding the atonement of Christ was the foundation of the

Stranraer Tailor's Theology

This view is best expressed in the doctrinal declaration of the Evangelical Union, which is as follows:

"As respects the *Nature of the Atonement,* we believe the Saviour's 'obedience unto death' to have been strictly vicarious or substitutionary, and to have constituted a propitiation or sacrificial satisfaction for the sins of men.

"Christ was treated as we deserved, that we

might be treated as He deserved; in which His obedience until death so fills the place of the sinner's punishment as to render the remission of sin's penalty morally possible and safe, and thus remove all legal barriers to the salvation of man; and on the ground of which, accordingly, God can be at once 'The just God and Saviour'—at once 'just, and the Justifier of him who believeth in Jesus.' This aspect of the atonement is vital to the blessed doctrine of man's justification, while yet a sinner, on the ground of the Saviour's merits, and through the free grace of God.

"As respects the *Extent of the Atonement,* we hold it to have been made for all men without distinction, exception, or respect of persons. We reject the modern dogma of a 'Double Reference' in the atonement—a special and efficacious reference to the elect, a general and inefficacious reference to the non-elect. What the atonement, as an atonement, was adapted and intended to accomplish for any, *that* it actually did accomplish for all for whom it was made—otherwise it was more than an atonement in relation to the one class, or less than an atonement in relation to the other. That 'Double Reference' scheme, as it is termed, owes its existence entirely to the necessities of a false or transitional theological position: it is an ambiguous provision for the special and temporary benefit of those who at present stand with one foot in Calvinism, and with the other beyond it. It is destitute of foundation either in Scripture or reason; and it sheds on the sinner, when on the very threshold of peace, the eclipse of a chilling and repelling doubt; for, by declaring that

Christ so died for the non-elect as to remove legal barriers to their salvation, but not so as to procure for them a converting influence of the Spirit, whereas He so died for the elect as infallibly to secure faith and final salvation, it leaves the returning sinner in hopeless perplexity as to whether, in the saving sense, Christ has died for him. In opposition to this notion, we hold that Christ's atonement wears the same plenary aspect to one and all for whom it was made; and that there lives not, nor ever lived in any age or clime, the human being for whom Christ did not shed His sin-expiating blood."

The eldest son of this worthy couple was born on December 13, 1846, and was named Alexander. His boyhood was that of the normal Scottish boy. Of these youthful days he was never inclined to say a great deal, but his fondness of a joke, even in old age, and the merry twinkle in his eye, were indications that when youth's impetuosity was untempered by experience and discretion he would be what is termed in Scotland, "a steerin' callant." Odd stories of boyish escapades, and a narrow escape from drowning, go to confirm the conjecture.

Being their first-born, the lad was in a special way the pride and the anxiety of his parents. He received careful instruction in spiritual things, and wise words of counsel from them, and he was also the subject of many prayers. Describing his home and his home training in after years, he wrote: "My parents were Christians, and I had the advantage of sound scriptural instruction in the things of God. I was cradled to sleep with the lullaby of psalms and hymns. My memory was stored with choicest portions of Scripture, and many a prayer was presented that I might be early led to acceptance of the Lord Jesus Christ."

Educational opportunities were not so plentiful then as now, but Alexander was given the best his parents could afford, and his schooling completed, he entered the office of David Guthrie, solicitor, Stranraer, where he remained until he was 18 years of age. The certificate of character he received from this worthy lawyer reads as follows:

"The bearer, Alexander Marshall, was in my office for two years. He is smart, courteous, obliging, steady, and trustworthy. His parents are very respectable, and he has also a very good character.

"(Signed) DAVID GUTHRIE, Writer."

A testimonial from the minister of the Church is also appended:

"I have very great pleasure in testifying to the character and conduct of Alexander Marshall.

"During the last eight years he has attended the Sabbath School in connection with my Church, and during that time has been under my own eye. I have formed a most favourable opinion of his habits of regularity and diligence and attention—ever conducting himself in a most creditable manner.

"He was also under my daily observation for about six months, when I had temporarily charge of the Stranraer Academy, and then also I had every reason to be highly gratified, while his industry and abilities were rewarded by his winning the silver

medal given to the best English scholar in that
Institution.

"I have every belief that he is in every way
truthful and trustworthy, and as he has been
accustomed to good habits of working, and knowing
him to be a sharp active lad, I can confidently
recommend him for employment in any business he
may turn his attention to.
(Signed) G.W. MATTHEWS, Minister Bridge St.
Church. Stranraer, 14th March, 1864."

The lure of the city, the desire to push his way in
the world, and his anxiety to taste the pleasures of
the time made him discontented with Stranraer.
With a mother's benediction, and followed by a
father's prayers, he set out for Glasgow, to be
apprenticed to the drapery trade. He entered the
warehouse of Arthur & Co., Queen Street, and
ultimately found himself in the silk department.
That he was a conscientious worker and enjoyed
the confidence of his employers was evidenced by
his being, after a period of years, made first hand in
his department.

For two years he sought what satisfaction he
could find in the gaiety and pleasure of the city.
Again and again he was deeply impressed with the
importance of becoming a Christian, but to quote
his own words: "I did not wish then to be saved. I
was anxious to enjoy a little more of the pleasures
and amusements of the world. The fact is, I was a
great coward. I was afraid if I became a Christian
my companions would call me a 'Revivalist,' or a
'praying hypocrite,' and I thought I could not stand
it. I had a secret conviction that if one became a

Christian he would have to give up pleasure and happiness." All the while the strivings of conscience and the yearnings of an unsatisfied heart rendered his life a burden, and the pleasures he longed for eluded his grasp.

A Striking Text

His convictions were deepened by hearing this striking text quoted: "He that being often reproved, hardeneth his neck, shall suddenly be destroyed, and that without remedy" (Prov. 29:1). Awakened to anxiety, he feared to venture, because he thought he could never hold on. It was in this frame of mind he entered a Circus in Ingram Street, Glasgow, where Gordon Forlong, a converted deist, was preaching. This preacher had the habit of repeating again and again striking statements regarding the truths of the Gospel.

What took place at that memorable meeting is best told in Mr. Marshall's own words:

"I thought he was a most extraordinary preacher. I can distinctly recollect him frequently repeating the words: 'It's the Blood that saves. It's the Blood that saves.' In showing that all that was necessary for the sinner's deliverance was completed by Christ on the Cross, he exclaimed: 'It's finished; it's finished; it's finished.' In thinking about salvation, my mind had been occupied with 'believing' instead of with the object of faith—Christ and His finished work. I imagined I believed, but not in the right way. The words, 'It is finished,' were carried home by the Holy Spirit to my heart and conscience. I asked myself, 'What is it that is finished?' I remembered the words were the dying words of the Lord Jesus (John 19:30). He explained the meaning of the wondrous statement, and showed that the sacrificial work had been completed—that Christ had 'put away sin by the sacrifice of Himself' (Heb. 9:26; John 1:29), and that every one who believed on Him was saved and had eternal life. Specially did he dwell on the blessed truth, that the very moment any one believed he was saved. 'He that believeth on Me hath everlasting life" (John 6:47). I had always supposed that I must feel some great change before I could be sure I was saved, and was continually looking into my heart to find peace.

"The preacher seemed to understand my difficulties, and explained that one must first believe on Jesus—and the feelings would follow. He clinched the truth by repeating again and again the following statement: 'Believing is the root, feeling is the fruit; believing is the root, feeling is the fruit.' The light from Calvary shone in upon my soul. I saw that Jesus had died in my stead and received sin's penalty, and that through believing the 'good news' made known to me in the Word I was saved and had everlasting life."

A Father's Counsel

Three letters written by his father at this time have been preserved by Mr. Marshall. The dates show that an intimate correspondence was kept up between father and son. They are entirely free from easy sentiment, but from beginning to end they breathe the spirit of true affection and earnest solicitude for the spiritual welfare of the son.

One of these letters, dated Jan. 30, 1865, reads: "DEAR SANDY,—We got your very gladdening letter this morning, and are glad to see from it that your mind has been led by the Good Spirit to see not only your deserts as a sinner, but the glorious simple truths that Jesus got what you deserved that you might be treated as if you had done no sin—in Scripture language you see—that He who knew no sin was made sin, that we might be made the righteousness of God in Him.

"Jesus never did sin, never felt sin, yet God treated Him as if He had sinned, that we who never felt good, never thought good; might be treated as if we were good. How simple, how Godlike—the plan of salvation neither by working nor feeling, but by Jesus alone; and its enjoyment just by believing or knowing it to be true. You in your note give a reason for your faith: the Word of God. The written Word of God, my son, is the only rock to build on. He tells no lies, and His written Word may be trusted. It is true that whosoever believeth on Jesus shall not perish. Rest on His Word. Thoughts will be thrust in upon your mind: 'Well, I am not saved; if I were saved I would do so-and-so; I would feel so-and-so, or I would not do so-and-so.' Remember our safety lies in Jesus, and when thoughts of such a nature arise, say to yourself: 'Well, I have done nothing, nor can do anything to save my soul, but Jesus has done it, done it all—and the Lord Jehovah is well pleased for His righteousness' sake. This righteousness was wrought out for me, and if God is well pleased with it what more do I need.'

"What did the Children of Israel need for safety that dreadful night when the destroying angel went through Egypt's land? Just the blood sprinkled on their door posts. God said: 'When I see the blood I will pass over you.'

"Their feelings had nothing to do with their safety. Not at all. No doubt they felt safe after they believed. Many put the cart before the horse. First feel, they say, and then believe. Such is not God's way. Believe, and as a consequence you will feel, and feel according to the nature or kind of truth believed. If saddening news be told one, they will feel sad after they believe it; if gladdening news, they will feel glad.

"With regard to experience, all men, and women, too, have different experiences when they first see God as He is revealed propitious; and before they see Him so too, one has one difficulty, another has another. Early training and constitutional tendencies have a great deal to do with the experiences of sinners both before and after they see the truth. Some ere they saw their safety in Jesus had scenes of difficulty to pass through; others again, like Lydia, from previous training were saved such depths of suffering. But notice, my son, the fault of such suffering lay with the parties themselves. Unbelief was the cause, and that alone. Trying may have to make a tower of good work to reach Heaven. Difficulties of a doctrinal nature have been used by Satan to keep sinners from their Saviour, in fact all kinds of difficulties drawn from all sources have been tried by the Devil to keep us from Him who says, 'Him that cometh to Me I will in no wise cast out,' and in proportion to the depth of their suffering, was their joy when they saw their safety in Jehovah Jesus ... John Bunyan's experience was different in degree from that of many who have as firmly trusted in the same Saviour. The clearer views one has on the evil of sin the better; the more will they hate it. The Cross supplies the fullest information about it—not Eden, not this present state of things on earth, not Hell itself, supplies us with one thousandth part of the evil of sin as Calvary does; and the clearer and more enlarged our views become of the wondrous work done there, the more will we hate that which crucified the Lord of Glory. Study your Bible more and more, my son, and may God keep you and make you useful."

In this remarkable letter we discover the good foundation the father laid for the edifice of Christian character and useful service which the son was to build up in the sixty-three years which were to follow.

CHAPTER II

Work and Witness

Those who enjoyed the friendship of Mr. Marshall know that there were never any half-measures with him, and this was characteristic of his Christian life. Confession of Christ followed conversion. His fellow-employees, including his master's son, afterwards Lord Glenarthur, heard from the young convert's lips of the dear Saviour he had found. His old companions were warned to flee from the wrath to come, and soon he was known by the names he formerly feared.

In the atmosphere of the Evangelical Union Church he found a spiritual nursery, and here were laid the foundations of the theology which characterised his preaching and teaching. Volumes in his library with portions underlined and annotated, from the pens of Morison, Ferguson, Adamson, Guthrie of Kendal, and other of the early leaders of that movement, give some indication of the care and thought he gave to such subjects as the nature and extent of the atonement, election, and the work of the Holy Spirit.

The effect of this painstaking study was afterwards made manifest in his sturdy presentation of the great doctrines of the Gospel, and his defence of the great truth that "Jesus by the grace of God tasted death for every man;" that God will have all men to be saved, and to come to a knowledge of the truth;

that Jesus gave Himself a ransom for all. Correspondence with a number of outstanding teachers which has been preserved by him gives us some idea of the forceful way in which he contended for what he considered to be fundamental to the whole

Plan of Salvation.

The following is a letter written to the Editor of *The Golden Lamp* on July 12, 1880:

"I am much surprised and disappointed at the reply given to the query: 'Is it right to say that Christ was the propitiation for the whole world?' in the July number of *The Golden Lamp*.

"Kindly allow me to give my reasons for dissenting from the conclusions of the writer. He says: 'Propitiation Godward is universal, as seen in the proclamation of pardon and salvation made to all; manwards it is by God made conditional on faith and acceptance.' Propitiation made conditional on faith and acceptance! Propitiation has been made and accepted by God 1800 years ago. There is nothing conditional about it. It was to God, not to man that propitiation was made. Man has nothing to do with the acceptance of the propitiation. He has to do with the acceptance or rejection of the pardon proclaimed to him on the ground of propitiation made. Propitiation has been accomplished, and a fact does not cease to be a fact because of man's acceptance or rejection of it. In the closing words of the reply I read, 'Godwards the atonement is universal in God's desire that all should come to repentance.' Is the extent of the atonement affected by man's accepting or rejecting salvation? The atonement is surely an accomplished fact, but the reply conveys the impression that the propitiation or atonement is something to be bestowed by God on man on condition of his acceptance of it. Again the writer says, 'Manwards it (the atonement) is limited by faith.' Then the extent of the atonement is necessarily dependent on man's belief! According to this a man cannot know that Christ died for him until he has the assurance of salvation. Hitherto I have believed that a man could not have the assurance of being saved without knowing that Christ died for him.

"The writer likewise asserts that to declare that the sins of the whole world are propitiated for would lead to universalism. This is, of course, tantamount to saying that every one whose sins are atoned for must necessarily be saved. Where is there Scripture for such a theory? What is the meaning of 1 John 2:1,2: 'He is the propitiation for our sins.' Whose sins? Believers. 'And not for ours only, but also for the whole world.' Surely the thought is that Christ is not merely the propitiation for the believers' sins, but for those of the whole world. Young translates it thus: 'He is a propitiation for our sins and not for ours only, but for those of the whole world.' Rotherham: 'He is a propitiation for our sins; not however for ours alone, but also for (those) of the whole world.' If, then, Christ is the propitiation for the sins of the whole world, could He be so apart from blood shedding? Could he be the propitiation for the sins of a single sinner without dying for such a one? It may, however, be contended that Christ is only a propitiation for the whole world—not for their sins. But if Christ is not a propitiation for their sins, what is He a propitiation or satisfaction for? If He is not a propitiation, or 'propitiatory sacrifice,' for their sins, is salvation possible to them? 'Without shedding of blood is no remission' (Heb. 9:22). If, however, there be a single sinner on the face of the earth for whom Christ's blood was not shed, is his salvation possible? Some have thought to evade the force of the word rendered 'propitiation' by translating it 'mercy seat.' I don't see what warrant there is for such alteration. The verb *hilaskomai* from which *hilasmos* comes means 'render propitious in respect to anything,' 'to expiate,' etc., and the only other place where *hilasmos* occurs in the New Testament is 1 John 4:10, and is rendered 'propitiation.' It has been asserted again and again, if Christ made atonement for the sins of all, then all must necessarily be saved. I have not yet seen a single passage that gives countenance to such an idea. On the contrary, I read that 'Christ died for all' (2 Cor. 5:15), 'tasted death for every man' (Heb. 2:9), 'gave Himself a ransom for all' (1 Tim. 2:6), gave His flesh for the life of the world (John 6:51). In John 3:17 we read: 'For God sent not His Son into the world to condemn the world, but that the world through Him might be saved.' Not that certain men must be saved for whom He died. This is shadowed forth in the paschal lamb. Though the lamb were slain no safety was secured apart from blood sprinkling, and no one's safety is secured apart from faith in Christ.

"In 1 Corinthians 15:1-3, Paul gives us a statement of the Gospel which he preached to the Corinthians, and by which they were saved: 'Moreover, brethren, I declare unto you the Gospel which I preached unto you, which also ye have received, and wherein ye stand: By which also ye are saved.' . . . 'For I delivered unto you first of all that which I also received, how that Christ died for our sins according to the Scriptures, and that He was buried and rose again the third day according to the Scriptures.' What then was the Gospel which Paul preached to the Corinthians when they were unsaved? 'Christ died for our sins' according to the Scriptures, and that He was buried and rose again the third day according to the Scriptures. The Gospel then which Paul preached, which the Corinthians believed, and by which they were saved, involved Christ's death for the person to whom it was proclaimed. It may be replied: 'Paul wrote to them as believers.' Granted, but the apostle is dealing with the Gospel which he preached to them while they were unbelievers. It must therefore have been true that Christ died for their sins whether they believed it or not.

"The Gospel is not an offer or an invitation, it is the positive statement of accomplished facts. All offers, however free, all invitations, however universal, are valueless when separated from the ground on which God bestows salvation on sinners.

"In another Scripture the apostle declares that, 'The Gospel is the power of God unto salvation to every one that believeth' (Rom. 1:16). What then is a sinner to believe in order to be saved? What was the Gospel that was preached unto the Corinthian sinners which was God's power unto their salvation? 'Christ died for our sins.' Believing that Christ died for the elect, for sinners, for the ungodly, won't give me peace. I must believe that He died for my sins, and if it is my duty to believe it, it must be true whether I believe it or not.

"And, last of all, if there is a single soul in this world whose sins are not atoned for, it is as absolutely impossible for that one to be saved as if he were already in Hell.

A.M."

The honoured servant who God used in his salvation was never forgotten by Mr. Marshall. To the end of life he spoke of Gordon Forlong with the respect and veneration which a son has for a father, but it was in his presentation of the Gospel that his regard for his spiritual parent was chiefly evident. The habit of reiteration, already referred to as one of the marks of Gordon Forlong's preaching, was one of the most distinct traits in Mr. Marshall's style of address. The memorable phrases which were so wonderfully blest to him that evening must have been repeated by him to thousands of listeners in all parts of the world. In clear ringing tones he would repeat again and again: "Believing is the root, feeling is the fruit," or, "God is satisfied with what Christ has done, why should you not be satisfied as well?"

Home Mission Effort

The opportunities for preaching which a new

movement like the Evangelical Union presented to
the zealous young Christian were eagerly laid hold
of. He was a director of its Home Mission effort,
and one of its most ardent preachers. The platforms
of the mission halls and the pulpits of not a few of
the young churches were opened to him, and with
acceptance and manifest blessing he exercised his
ministry. He was a member of Dundas Street
Church, and enjoyed the friendship of Dr. Morison,
of Dr. Kirk, the author of *Papers on Health*, and other
noteworthy members of the movement.

That his earnestness and zeal raised the ire of the
forces of evil, and that the young preacher suffered
for the Gospel is evidenced by the following extract
from the *Daily Mail* (Glasgow) of 23rd July, 1872:

Street Preacher Assaulted

"An open-air meeting was held in Dobbie's Loan,
at the corner of Ann Street, Port-Dundas, on Friday
evening, under the superintendence of Mr. Weir,
missionary in connection with the Mission Hall in
Water Street, carried on under the auspices of the
Mission Board of North Dundas Street E.U.
Church (Rev. Dr. Morison's). Mr. Weir had just
finished his address when he intimated that Alex.
Marshall, a member of the Mission Board, would
supplement what he had said by saying a few
words. Mr. Marshall gave out a hymn, which was
just about finished, when three men pushed their
way through the crowd, and made straight for the
speaker. One of them (McGrorty) walked behind
the speaker, and another right before him.
McGrorty, without any warning, struck Mr.

Marshall a heavy blow with his clenched fist, knocking him to the ground. This was the signal for a general attack on Mr. Marshall. Another of the group threw a brick at the preacher's head, narrowly missing him, and striking McGrorty on the eye. Mr. Marshall succeeded in disentangling himself from the grasp of his assailant, and proceeded down Ann Street, where he was seized by another man, knocked to the ground, and again struck. By this time a large crowd had collected, and he was rescued from their grasp. The prisoner McGrorty was apprehended on Saturday afternoon and committed to prison, but was liberated on bail. He failed to answer the charge when called yesterday at the Northern Police Court. Not a single word was used by Mr. Weir, the missionary, fitted to arouse the animosity of any. We may add that open-air meetings have been held in the neighbourhood for the last five years."

All the while Alexander Marshall was daily engaged in the drapery warehouse, meriting the approval of his employers, and steadily working his way toward the position of responsibility which he ultimately occupied. Another employee of this firm was at the same time showing the same steadfast zeal in the service of Christ. Alice Todd, an enthusiast for Christ, who afterwards became Mrs. Todd Osborne, was just commencing what proved to be her life work among the soldiers in the Old Barracks in the Gallowgate, and found a ready helper in Alexander Marshall.

D.L. Moody's Visit to Glasgow

In the year 1874 D.L. Moody and Ira D. Sankey visited Glasgow, and a real wave of blessing went across the city. The foundations of evangelistic activities which were features of Glasgow's religious life were laid at this time, and it was Mr. Marshall's privilege to share in that great movement. He was a valued helper in the after-meetings, and pointed many to the Saviour. He was introduced to Mr. Moody by Dr. Morison, who writes of him as follows:

"The bearer, Mr. Alexander Marshall, though still quite a young man, has been, for many years, a consistent and devoted disciple of Jesus. He has all along been eager to engage in 'works of faith and labours of love.' I consider him well qualified, both from principle and from experience, to be helpful to inquirers. JAMES MORISON, D.D. March 18, 1874."

The necessary ticket was granted, and bears the signature of Andrew Bonar.

It was a bitter disappointment to Mr. Marshall's friends that he steadfastly refused to enter the Theological Hall of the E.U. Church and prepare for the ministry, but other influences were leading him into the path of service in which the greater part of his life was spent. John R. Caldwell, a young man of nearly his own age, the son of Wm. Caldwell, silk manufacturer, Glasgow, was also led to a knowledge of the truth through the ministry of Gordon Forlong. As a result of deep spiritual exercise, Mr. Caldwell's father and some others were led to meet on the simple lines indicated in the opening chapters of the Acts of the Apostles. They practised the baptism of believers, they met on the first day of the week to break bread, and when they did so they waited in humble dependence on the risen Head of the Church for guidance and for ministry. Singularly, Mr. Marshall, by the study of the New Testament, was finding himself being guided in a similar way, and as their paths lay together, Mr. Marshall joined himself to the little company of disciples meeting then in a hall in West Campbell Street, Glasgow. This step did not mean a narrowing of his sympathies, for in the early simplicity of those days, the subtle distinctions which lead to the setting up of sectarian barriers were unknown, and men were loved and welcomed because they belonged to Christ.

In Many Activities

Having for his associates John R. Caldwell, Alexander Stewart, Robert Kerr, William Quarrier, W.D. Dunn, D.J. Findlay, and many other honoured servants of Christ, most of whom have gone to their reward, Alexander Marshall gave himself up to the work of the Gospel. A pulpit could always be got at a street corner, and Mr. Marshall's style of preaching being eminently suited for the open air, he seldom failed to attract an audience. But his activities were not confined to the open air. Music Halls and Public Halls were hired; wherever there was an open door the glad tidings were carried. Many were the trophies of grace won in those far-off days. On Saturday evenings he would take the lead in a small, homely Bible reading with young Christians, who had been invited to tea in a brother's house.

Distance was no barrier, and it was nothing for the preachers, after a day at the counter or desk, to walk the seven miles to Hamilton, or some similar centre, to preach to the waiting audiences which could be gathered at that time. However, such strenuous activity began to have its effect, and a threatened break down in health caused Mr. Marshall to reconsider the whole position.

A Great Decision

The demands made upon his time and energy, the open doors for the Gospel message, and the insistent urge of the love of Christ were such that it was impossible to continue in business and at the same time fulfil what the Spirit of God was clearly indicating as his vocation. The choice was made, and he was led of God to relinquish a business career and give himself wholly to the work of the Gospel. When it is remembered that eleven years passed between the date of his conversion and this decision (years filled to the utmost with activity in the service of the Lord), it will be seen that the choice was not lightly made nor the decision hastily arrived at.

His untiring energy, his integrity, his persistence, and his more than ordinary general ability marked him out for a successful business career, and it was no easy thing to step aside from it and renounce earthly prospects and an assured income, to become an itinerant evangelist. After his decision was made, his intimate friend, Mr. Caldwell, asked him to join him in his business, but Mr. Marshall's reply was: "I have just decided I must give my whole time to the Lord for the work of the Gospel." Mr. Caldwell's reply was just as characteristic of the man: "Not another word, Alex., that settles it."

Early Simplicity

Companies of Christians meeting in New Testament simplicity were few in number, and mostly scattered over wide areas. The saints making up the local Assemblies were neither wealthy nor influential, and nothing was being done to secure outward unity. Thus it happened that Alexander Marshall stepped out in the service of the Lord, without any visible means of support, without committee or organisation to look after his interests, and with no guarantee save that which God gives to all His people, "My God shall supply all your need" (Phil. 4:19).

It is not to be supposed, however, that he failed to seek the fellowship of those Christians with whom he had been associated. Following the apostolic example the saints in Hope Hall, Glasgow, met, and after prayer commended our brother to the Lord for the work to which He had called him. His two friends, Alexander Stewart and J.R. Caldwell, publicly by the laying on of hands, identified themselves with him in his going forth. The letter of commendation which he received, signed by these worthy men, is reproduced below as evidence of the simplicity and sincerity which marked the beginnings in Scotland of what is known as assemblies of Christians gathered to the name of the Lord:

"Glasgow, 3rd August, 1877.

DEAR BROTHER,—As you wish from us a letter of commendation, we have pleasure in stating that you have long been known to us as a brother in Christ and a labourer in the Gospel, and we gladly commend you to the help and fellowship of Christians to whom we may be known in the places you visit in seeking to do the Lord's work.

When in Glasgow you are recognised as in fellowship with the Assembly meeting in Clarendon Hall there.

We are, brother, truly yours in Christ Jesus our Lord.

(Signed) JOHN R. CALDWELL.
A. STEWART."

Never in all the long years which followed did Alexander Marshall utter one word of regret regarding the choice he had made. Never was he heard to complain regarding the support he received, never did he boast of what he might have been, or speak of having made any sacrifice for the Lord. His constant theme was the love and unfailing goodness of God, and if at any time he spoke of himself it was to extol the Lord's mercy to him, His unworthy servant.

Good Advice

Entering the private room of the Editor of *The Witness* (HyP) just after an evangelist, known for his grumbles concerning money, had been giving one of his doleful accounts of the small amount left after railway fares had been paid, the Editor inquired: "How is it, Mr. Marshall, we never hear you speak about money?" A.M. replied: "When I went out, Rice T. Hopkins gave me a piece of advice which I have followed." "Now, if it is not asking too much, would you tell me what it was." "He said, 'Marshall, if you get too much say nothing. If you get too little, say the same.'"

"Well," replied the Editor, "you have certainly kept to it, for all the 30 and more years I have known you, I have never had the slightest hint either way, except when you were asking for $5 bills to send to a backwoods worker in Canada. I then judged you had something to spare."

It was for years a common request, that the firm should save $1 and $5 bills sent in payment of accounts, for A.M. to return to lonely workers in the land from whence they came.

A Door of Utterance

The young evangelist set one principle before him which he never let go. He determined if God was leading him out, that he would wait until God opened the doors. To him dependence upon God not only entailed waiting upon Him for supplies, but also waiting upon Him for service. This did not mean idleness, or weeks of resting (a phrase used in another sphere to cover unemployment), and which is unfortunately not infrequently used by some now giving their whole time to the work of the Gospel. There was no established circle of meetings to which a preacher could go in rotation, but doors were opened nevertheless. The fact is, that in those days the sphere of the evangelist was recognised to be the world, that wherever there was a sinner it was the business of the evangelist to carry to him the Gospel message, and wherever people would lend an ear to that message and afford an opportunity for its proclamation, Alexander Marshall and those early brethren went.

Fellowship in the Gospel was very real with those simple-minded saints, and when the evangelist stretched out to new ground, funds were forthcoming to pay for the hire of halls, where schoolhouses and similar buildings were not available.

In this way the truths of the Lord's Coming for His saints, the priesthood of all believers, the unity of the Church, and the blessedness of gathering together in New Testament simplicity were carried with the Gospel message to many districts and towns in Scotland and England where, as an outcome, companies of Christians now carry on a vigorous testimony.

In the course of this itinerary, Mr. Marshall met and served in the Gospel with many loved and honoured servants of God long since called to their rest and reward. Donald Ross, Rice T. Hopkins, Henry Moorhouse, John Hambleton, John G. McVicker, Richard and Cecil Hoyle, John Morley,

Donald Munro, John Smith, Harrison Ord, Wm. Lincoln, R.C. Chapman and Chas. Morton are among the best known, but many other faithful and godly men, whose names are not so familiar, found in him a true yokefellow in the Gospel.

Details of these early movements are now difficult to obtain, for most of those who took part in them are no longer with us.

These labours extended from Shetland to Cornwall. Very few towns and districts in Great Britain but were touched at that time. Theatres and places of entertainment were hired for the Sunday evenings, and large audiences were brought together, when remarkable scenes were witnessed. The frequency with which, after the lapse of fifty years, those who move among Assemblies of Christians, meet those who were brought to the Lord through Mr. Marshall's ministry in these early days is evidence of how real and widespread was the work of grace.

The following personal testimony of Mr. D.J. Findlay is of special interest:

"I knew A.M. well in 1874 and onward for some years. In later years I saw little of him, but always retained a high regard for him, and from first to last we were 'Alick' and 'David' when we met.

When Moody left Glasgow in the summer of 1875 a Committee of young men was appointed to carry on the great Young Men's Meetings. I think A.M. was one of this Committee.

In July-September, 1874, I conducted week-end services in Dunoon, which God made a very wonderful blessing. One Sunday in July 'Alick' came to our help, and of that day we have a very vivid recollection. The afternoon was spent studying provision a little book, *'Trust in the Living Father,'* which Henry Varley had just published. At night in a crowded hall 'Alick' gave a burning message, commencing with often used words: 'Fellow-travellers on the road to Eternity,' and with repeated appeals, 'Young man, where will you spend Eternity?' Hundreds were brought to Christ through these meetings."

CHAPTER III

Pioneering in Canada

News began to reach this country of the conditions existing among the settlers in the Canadian provinces, and of the need of Gospel work among them. Pictures of the rough shacks of fifty years ago convey some idea of the primitive those hardy settlers made for shelter from the severities of the Canadian climate. Provision for the spiritual needs was on the same scanty footing. A few Gospel pioneers such as Donald Munro, John Smith, and later Donald Ross, had gone from Scotland to spread the good news, and information sent home by them stirred Alexander Marshall to action. Believing he had the call of God, he sailed from Liverpool for New York on December 24th, 1879, on the S.S. "Italy," the journey occupying about twelve days of rough sailing. He was received into the house of R.W. Owens, New York, and enjoyed the hospitality of Mr. and Mrs. Owens for a short time. Early in January he went north to Hamilton, Ontario, to be present at a gathering of believers, and was warmly welcomed by that band of pioneers, which included Donald Ross, Donald Munro, John Smith, James Campbell, and J.M. Carnie.

These devoted men welcomed another worker who was prepared to "break up the prairie and be content with bed, board, and washing" (a phrase often used by Donald Ross) as material compensation. From necessity as well as from choice the preachers were pioneers. Assemblies were few and far between, and if souls were to be won new ground must be broken up. They lived among the people, they lived with the people, shared their hardships, and fared as they fared. Fellowship in the Gospel, and with the worker, was on apostolic lines, and gifts were more frequently in kind that in coin. The scanty shelter from the rigours of winter meant enduring much hardship, hair and beard being sometimes frozen when they awoke in the morning, but they were full of the joy of the Lord, and these things were made light of, provided they could carry the message of salvation to the needy, and be the means of pointing some sinner to the Saviour.

The new arrival threw himself into the work with all the vigour his ardent nature was capable of. In the city of Toronto he found a vast field for service for the first year of his stay in Canada. Interest in the Gospel was manifest, and the simplicity which marked preaching and practice enabled these pionerers to enter open doors. The good news was carried by them wherever a sinner was open to receive it.

An Interesting Letter

Twelve months after his arrival in Canada a letter from his pen, describing the Annual Believers' Meetings in Hamilton appeared in the *Northern*

Witness. From this we have culled the following brief notes.

"The Believers' Annual Meetings, held in this city on the 13th, 14th, 15th, and 16th of the present month, have been times of refreshing from the Lord, and souls, we believe, throughout eternity will praise Him for strength and encouragement received. The attendance was considerably larger than last year; and it was very cheering to find brethren and sisters in the Lord from the United States and various parts of Canada thus coming together. One brother, an ex-Presbyterian preacher, came from the western part of the State of Iowa, a distance of 900 miles. The meetings began at 10 o'clock on Thursday morning, and finished on Sunday evening. Most of the forenoon was devoted to prayer and praise.

"An address was given on 'The Judgment Seat of Christ,' by A. Marshall. It was stated that we were creatures of extremes, that like the pendulum of the clock, we oscillated from one extreme to the other, unless our minds and hearts were regulated and controlled by God's Word. We are all familiar with one of the 'faithful sayings' (1 Tim. 1:15) mentioned by the Apostle Paul, but are we not often unmindful and forgetful of another? 'This is a faithful saying, and these things I will that thou affirm constantly, that they which have believed in God might be careful to maintain good works' (Titus 3:8). We love to think of, and dwell upon, the blessed truth, that there is no condemnation to them that are in Christ Jesus; but do we as often meditate upon the solemn and momentous fact, that every saved soul shall yet have to give account of himself to God (Rom. 14:12); that we must all be manifested before the judgment-seat of Christ (2 Cor. 5:10; Rom. 14:10); that then the Lord will bring to light the hidden things of darkness, and make manifest the counsels of the heart? (1 Cor. 4:5). We will then be manifested in the full blaze of the light of His holiness. Motives, feelings, and actions will then be tested.

"Now there is so much of self and sin mingled with our holiest deeds that we cannot properly estimate them. So much hypocrisy; so much profession and so little manifestation; so much high talking and low walking. Oftentimes we don't wish to weigh our actions and test our motives. We have our eye so filled with ourselves, and so much on circumstances, that we do not see the crookedness of our ways, or know the perversity of our hearts. Then we shall know, even as we are known. Everything will then be tested. 'The fire shall try every man's work of what sort it is' (1 Cor. 3:13). All our Christless service, our open and secret backslidings, our obstinancy and rebellion, our pride and selfishness will be manifested to us. The wood, hay , and stubble will be burned up, but the gold, silver, and precious stones will be purified. 'If any man's work abide he shall receive a reward, if any man's work shall be burned he shall suffer loss' (1 Cor. 3:14,15). The rewards spoken of for faithfulness were briefly referred to, and believers exhorted to live in view of the judgment-seat of Christ.

Blessing the Gospel

"The evening Gospel Meeting was held in the Grand Opera House, which was crowded in every corner, hundreds having to be turned away, and an overflow meeting held in the open-air. Above 1600 people were present. The meeting was addressed by brethren Ross, Smith, and others, and was a very encouraging one. Numbers were spoken to who seemed anxious about their souls, and a few have turned up at the Gospel meetings now being held in the city, who profess to have found peace. On Monday most of the friends from a distance left by the various trains, and at the depot hymns were sung, much to the astonishment, and, we trust, to the benefit of other travellers.

"Another brother and myself have been preaching in the city for the past seven weeks. On Lord's day last we spoke in the Grand Opera House. Hundreds had to be turned away, and the doors closed. I ask the prayers of the readers of *The Witness* for the Lord's work in Canada and the United States, that many labourers may be thrust forth, and that those who are already in the harvestfield may be kept in close communion with the Lord, and be better fitted to sound forth the praises of Him who has called them out of darkness into the marvellous light."

It is noticeable that the preaching of the Gospel occupied a considerable part of these gatherings. In those days Christians spoke of salvation to their friends and neighbours, and used every effort to get them under the sound of the Evangel of Christ.

Many were brought to the Lord as the result of

this special effort. The interest and blessing continued for weeks after the evangelists had left.

Mr. Marshall's colleague of those days, Mr. Richard Irving, tells the story of 1881 as follows:

"Another Life Choice

"Towards the end of January, 1881, I started north, and spent a month in St. Louis, and about the same time in Pittsburg and Harrisburg.

"After this I joined David Hughes in Blackrock, near Buffalo, and together we crossed the border into Canada, halting at St. Catherines then proceeding to Hamilton. There I first met our esteemed and beloved brother, Alex. Marshall. He had been preaching for months in Orillia, and he spoke of real openings for the Gospel in that vicinity, and urged us to go there.

"Not many days after we arrived in Orillia, and found many young converts, and an Assembly formed of over 60 in fellowship. On January 1st there had been no Assembly, meeting in the Lord's Name alone, and receiving all true members of Christ's body; then in the month of May over 60 were gathered together, bearing no sectarian name. This number of converts did not represent all saved by the Gospel preached by Marshall and others; possibly a far greater number were savingly converted who never identified themselves with this company. The whole district around Orillia was stirred by the Gospel preached with freshness, joy, and power. The movement was given publicity by the press in censure and commendation, and this brought the people from far and near to hear what was regarded as 'the new doctrine.'

"Excursions were made into different parts of the surrounding country, and we were always seeing signs following the preached Word.

"Notably at Seven Bridge, a village fifteen miles north of Orillia, blessing followed in the form of genuine converts, who were not left to drift, but were instructed in the things which accompany salvation. Thus the believers being established and confirmed in the faith, in due course an Assembly was formed in Seven Bridge on the same scriptural lines.

"In the month of June a Gospel Tent was pitched in the village of Warminster, seven miles from Orillia, and meetings continued nightly until late in September. The interest in the tent meetings was widespread, and the tent was crowded. In many instances whole families in that community were saved. A conservative estimate of the number of genuine conversions under that canvas tent would be 100. The work was followed up with instruction as to the believer's security, the two natures, the Coming of the Lord, and the ordinances. As a result an Assembly was formed.

"During that year brother Marshall baptised over 200 professed believers, and some more were baptised by the other helpers.

"In the fall of the same year, brother Marshall found an opening in Hobart, fifteen miles from Orillia. The people responded to the Gospel preached nightly for weeks by brother Marshall and myself. A goodly number were saved, and the converts were led on and instructed about their relationship to God and the world. Helpful Bible readings were conducted upon such subjects as: The Holy Spirit, The One Body, New Testament Teaching about the Church of God, and What Constitutes a Local Church or Assembly. The outcome was that another company was formed.

"We have outlined the formation of four companies or Assemblies, the product of the Gospel preached by brother Marshall, and the others named, in the year 1881. These other helpers, no doubt under God, contributed much to the success of the work. Still it is only fair to say that the chief aggressive force in this stirring movement was Mr. Marshall.

"It is worthy of note that these Assemblies were comprised almost entirely of young converts, and bore a striking resemblance to the New Testament pattern.

"This is a brief summary of the work carried on during one year, and the approximate results. It was pioneer work, as, at that time there was no Assembly north of Toronto. The Gospel was preached in the open air, and at various fairs in the fall, and tracts were distributed by the thousands, so that almost every home covering a wide district possessed our literature.

"His love for the Gospel made him think about it, write about it, live it, and preach it, and in such a way as, in our circle of acquaintance, we have not seen excelled."

His Marriage

In the year 1882, Mr. Marshall was united in marriage to Miss Amy Florence Tate. He had been instrumental in helping Miss Tate's brother spiritually, and as Miss Tate had been led to the Lord as a result of a word spoken to her by the late Mr. J.G. McVicker some time before coming to Orillia, she readily joined in the spiritual work which was then going on. Friendship ripened into affection, and a suitable and happy union was thus formed. For forty-six years his devoted wife shared with him the joys and the sacrifices and sorrows inseparable from the work of an evangelist. Their mutual love for the Lord and trust in each other, enabled Mrs. Marshall almost from the first day of their married life to forgo the claims she might have had on her husband's time and companionship, provided he could thus reach the needy with the message of life.

After a short visit to the Homeland they returned to Toronto and made their home in that city. A period of great activity in the Gospel followed. There was a real awakening of spiritual interest; sinners were seeking their way to the Saviour, and saints were seeking to know the will of God more fully. Mr. and Mrs. Marshall found their hands full. Their home was open for the Lord's servants, their afternoons were given to visiting the anxious, and their evenings to the preaching of the Gospel.

The story of 1883 is best told by Mr. Richard Irving, Mr. Marshall's colleague:

"For some time urgent invitations reached Mr. Marshall from two business men, Messrs. Haines and Lockett, of Belleville, Ont., to visit that city. They rented the Metropolitan Hall, with a seating capacity for six or seven hundred. In February of 1883, Mr. Marshall reached Belleville and began meetings—these meetings were continued nightly for seven or eight weeks. George Grove spent three weeks with Mr. Marshall, and the remainder of the time Richard Irving was associated with our brother.

"God gave much blessing, and over fifty were added to the little Assembly, among them Dr. Andrews, better known as Mrs. Cyril Bird, the author of *Little is Much if God is in It*. Belleville became the parent Assembly of four or five others in that section of Ontario.

"In the summer of the same year, brethren Marshall and Irving pitched a tent in Guelph for some weeks; a few souls were saved and gave evidence of salvation in after life. As the interest was not enthusiastic, Mr. Marshall took the tent to London, Ont., for the rest of the season, with better results.

"In November of the same year brethren Marshall and Irving began meetings in Rugby, a good farming section, a short distance from Orillia. The Gospel was preached nightly for about eight weeks, to most interested audiences; the whole district was stirred. As many as 100 people, mostly inquirers, would remain after 10 o'clock to hear more about God's way of Salvation. Not less than 75 professed conversion. Here it was that the late Arthur E. Hodgkinson received Christ, and afterwards became a useful servant of our Lord."

CHAPTER IV

Fruitful and Happy Years

Suitable literature to place in the hands of inquirers and young converts was difficult to obtain. To overcome this difficulty, Mr. Marshall set apart a room in his house as a bookroom, and imported books and tracts from Great Britain, in order that workers and inquirers might be supplied. During his itinerant missions Mrs. Marshall attended the bookroom, combining the duties of housewife, book steward, and secretary. There was little time to murmur or complain, but there was no need to do either. The joy of the Lord was filling their hearts, and they were having the unspeakable privilege of leading souls to the Saviour. This more than compensated for wearied minds and bodies.

Tent work in the province of Ontario led them to remove their home to Orillia, which soon became a strategic centre from which to reach the villages and settlements on Lake Ontario. Halls, barns, schools and kitchens were used, and filled by men and women anxious to hear the good news. Many were brought to the Lord at that time who in turn took up the Gospel story, and have been spared to labour for many years for the Lord. Among them were S.W. Benner, G. Benner, Mr. and Mrs. J.A. Orton.

Teaching the Converts

After a period of special meetings in which many professed, one of the ministers asked Mr. Marshall what he proposed to do with the converts. His answer was characteristic: "Teach them to observe all things." "What does that mean?" was the further question. "Baptism, the priesthood of all believers, breaking of bread, separation from evil." The taking of this definite stand alienated a number, but Mr. Marshall went on seeking to practise what he believed, and the Lord continued to bless the testimony and add to the number of the saved.

In order that our readers may fully appreciate the conditions, we quote from a letter of Mr. Marshall's dated 11th October, 1882.

"Labourers are beset by difficulties and trials on every hand. Breaking up fresh ground is not easy, but it is delightful work. Those who are called to this service need much courage, faith, and patience. They must also be willing to 'endure hardness as good soldiers of Christ Jesus,' and count on being misunderstood, misrepresented, and maligned. Into whatever town, hamlet, or village they enter, they are met by the cry: 'Why come here? There are plenty of churches and ministers.'

"It cannot be questioned that there are many 'churches' and 'ministers' in Canada and in the States; but, alas, amidst the profession that abounds, few there are, comparatively speaking, who can give 'a reason for the hope that is within them.' Whenever the Gospel is told out in freshness, simplicity, and power, the cry is raised: 'Heresy! heresy!' One minister where I laboured for a considerable time declared that 'simply believing on the Lord Jesus might do for the days of the apostles, but would not do now.'

"When evangelists go to districts, and preach in halls or schoolhouses, taking with them an open Bible, teaching the young converts what God has taught them, they are accused of being 'breakers up of the churches' and 'sowers of division,' and the people are warned to beware of them. More labourers are much needed. There is a wide and open door all throughout Canada and the States for the preaching of the Gospel. There is much land to be possessed. Young men who have a heart for God and for souls, and who are fitted for preaching the Gospel, would find a splendid field for service."

Mr. Marshall's sojourn in the province of Ontario extended to seven years. During the larger portion of that time the district of Orillia was his parish. It remained unto the end his first love. It occupied the premier place in his affections, and the bond of sympathy which existed between him and the saints in Orillia and district was one of the loveliest things in his remarkable life. In all the vicissitudes of a life not altogether free from struggle and conflict, he found help and consolation in fellowship with the band of men and women who by his instrumentality were brought to a knowledge of the truth. One of the bitterest experiences of his life was the alienation of some of these believers during a period of controversy concerning fellowship a few years ago.

Circulating the Truth

It was in Orillia that two things by which he will be most remembered took shape. The book room which he opened when in Toronto was enlarged when he removed to Orillia, its usefulness extended, and from it, supplies of useful Gospel literature began to circulate across the continent. Mr. Marshall's pen also began to be requisitioned for the supply of Gospel articles, and the Gospel arrow feathered by a striking story and pictorial illustration flowed steadily from the press. A monthly magazine, *The Gospel Herald*, with articles brief and bright, yet full of the Gospel, was established. The magazine attained a considerable circulation, and with the Book Store continued to function until a few years ago, when the establishment of importing houses for evangelical literature in Toronto, and the advanced years of Mr. S.W. Benner, who carried on the business after Mr. Marshall left Orillia, seemed to indicate that their period of service was at an end.

As the companies of Christians in this district grew in grace and experience, Mr. Marshall felt that his presence in the district was no longer necessary, and the call of the West led him to move out to the Pacific seaboard. Following a farewell tea, when they were commended to the Lord, Mr. and Mrs. Marshall left Orillia on September 20th, 1889. Mr. Marshall's graphic description of the journey is most interesting, and the information given gives some idea of the remarkable development of Canada in the present century. Winnipeg had 20,000 inhabitants, Vancouver 14,000 and Calgary was not sufficiently important to merit more than passing mention; now these are vast and important cities.

On the Pacific Seaboard

As an indication of the activities of the saints at that time, the following is instructive:

"I also spent a night at Selkirk, a town on the Red River, twenty miles east of Winnipeg. An Assembly of believers, fifteen to twenty in fellowship, sustain an active and aggressive Gospel work among the halfbreeds, Indians, and white people. A Chippewa chief is in their fellowship, likewise his son, an intelligent Government school teacher, recently saved. The latter, on the night of my visit, addressed the people who were mostly Cree and Chippewa Indians and halfbreeds, in Cree, and I followed in English.

"The chief's son appears to be an earnest, humble Christian worker; he can speak fluently in Cree, Chippewa, and English. Attempts have been made to secure his services in the interest of a sect, but hitherto he has persistently refused to entertain any such proposals. One of the brethren in the Selkirk Assembly (formerly in fellowship in London, England) is deeply interested in the welfare of the Indians, and purposes giving up his business in order to take a Government school (Indian), and devote his spare time to looking after their spiritual welfare. There are tens of thousands of Indians in Canada who are as ignorant of the Gospel of Christ as the inhabitants of Central Africa."

In Vancouver only eight came together to break bread. The company in Victoria numbered twenty on the Sunday morning the visitors were present. San Francisco was reached on October 5th, and the third annual conference took place on October 8th. Those were the days of small things, and the Assembly mustered only about forty-five, many of them saved as the result of the labours of that faithful pioneer, Donald Ross. A spell of Gospel meetings conducted by Mr. Marshall and J. Goodfellow followed the conference. Of San Francisco Mr. Marshall says:

"This is the most openly ungodly city I was ever in. Theatres and saloons are in full blast on the Lord's Days. Stores are opened and men are to be seen on all hands working."

The following report of the extended tour of the Pacific Coast was supplied by Mr. Marshall at the time:

"Brother Goodfellow and I laboured together for about ten weeks in San Francisco, holding nightly meetings in the Gospel Hall, 826 Howard Street, a nice large room in a central locality, and used now by the Assembly for their regular meetings. The weeknight meetings were at first poorly attended, but steadily increased, while on Lord's Days the hall was usually well filled, and our open-air services were most encouraging.

"Unlike New York, Boston, and other large American cities, no 'permit' is necessary to preach in the open-air. We were greatly cheered in being privileged to see large numbers of men standing for a length of time listening attentively to the proclamation of 'the Old, Old Story,' within a few yards of the principal business thoroughfares of the city. Our open-air audiences were largely composed of young men, of whom there are sixty-five thousand between the ages of sixteen and thirty-five in San Francisco. Many nationalities were represented, including Spaniards, Cubans, Italians, French, German, Scandinavians, Chinese, and Japanese.

"On leaving San Francisco, brother Goodfellow and I went to Santa Cruz, a beautiful watering place about eighty miles south of San Francisco, where there is a little company who meet solely in the Lord's Name. After remaining there a few days, I returned north, leaving brother Goodfellow to continue the meetings. San Francisco is a remarkable city. Forty years ago it was a Mexican village, and now it is a great commercial centre, with an estimated population of 330,000 souls; of this number over eighty per cent are foreigners, who themselves or their parents were born outside of the United States.

"Among Japanese and Chinese

"Among its mixed and multifarious nationalities, there are thousands of Japanese. I had a most interesting conversation with a young Japanese man in the Gospel Hall, at the close of one of our meetings. Professing to be saved, and giving Scripture for it, I asked what denomination he belonged to. He immediately replied, 'Me no believe in denominations; me a disciple of Jesus.' I could not help wishing that all God's people were of the same mind. He informed us that six other Japanese youths joined with him every week night, after business hours, in studying the Scriptures together.

"The Chinese are much better represented than the Japanese; the estimated population of 'Chinatown' being 40,000. 'Chinatown' is the name given to the Chinese quarters in the cities on the Pacific coast. It is a most interesting sight to take a walk through 'Chinatown,' although the olfactory organs are usually greeted with unsavoury odours. Several of us were conducted through 'Chinatown' late one night by an experienced guide. Gambling dens are in full operation; but it is difficult for the police to apprehend the culprits, as there is always a man watching without, and another within, to give the alarm if any of the officers appear. The opium dens were packed with people in their little bunks, occupied in smoking the deadly drug. It saddened us to see the number of victims of this fascinating vice.

"We visited several of their 'Joss' houses, or temples, and saw the various gods which they profess to fear, if not worship. The Chinese New Year opened when we were there. This is a great event to John Chinaman. Debts are paid at the end of each year. Rather than begin the New Year in debt, a Chinaman will sell his furniture, beg, borrow, or steal. The year must be 'rounded,' else they fear that the wicked devils will hurt them. At the 'Joss' houses, lights were kept burning, and also in dwelling-houses, to keep the evil spirits away. Fire-crackers were discharged with a deafening noise for the same purpose. Stores and houses were gaily decked with flags and bunting, and lanterns were seen on all hands. The Chinese on the Pacific Coast are, as a rule, an industrious, inoffensive, hard-working class of people. This is a great field for young men who have the desire to work at their trades or occupations, and at the same time serve the Lord in using their leisure hours in working among the Japanese or Chinese.

"The Problem of Nationality

"A poll-tax of fifty dollars per head is imposed on every Chinaman that lands on the continent. American workmen look upon Chinese labour with great jealousy. The Chinese can live on so much less than Americans or Britishers; and their advent to the continent is considered by many a curse. Notices like the following are often seen: 'None but white labour employed.' It is a serious problem, this question of Chinese immigration, and wise hands are needed at Washington and Ottawa to direct and guide in such a delicate and difficult subject. Japanese immigration is not restricted, and no poll-tax is levied. They conform to the customs of the country, dress like Americans, buy, sell, and trade as others. A Chinaman, on the other hand, does not consider himself an American or Canadian citizen, will not conform to the customs of the people, and proclaims by his dress, habits, and speech, that he is a 'pilgrim and a stranger,' piling up his treasures in China, whither he hopes to follow as soon as he can. What a lesson for those who propose to be citizens of Heaven!

"Victoria is a contrast to San Francisco. Indifference to the things of God and eternity may be said to characterise Western American cities, whilst in most of the Canadian centres of population, formal, outward religion is the barrier to the spread of the Gospel."

The tour of the West included visits to and special missions in Los Angeles, Vera Cruz, Portland, Seattle, New Westminster, Vancouver, and Victoria, and in each of these places fruit remains from the seed sown at that time.

A return visit was paid to Orillia, and afterwards Mr. and Mrs. Marshall set sail for the Homeland, where they arrived in August, 1890. This completed a period of service and fellowship in the Gospel that Mr. Marshall looked upon as one of the most fruitful and happiest in his long and useful career.

CHAPTER V

The Defence and Confirmation of the Gospel

The evangelist may change his sphere of labour, but wherever he is he practises his vocation. Mr. Marshall on his return to Scotland found open doors waiting for him to enter, and he was again engaged in itinerant Gospel work. He was in the prime of life, and in the enjoyment of good health, and spared not himself in the service. He toured the country from North to South, never arranging a great distance ahead, and always leaving himself free to remain in a place as long as there were signs of the Spirit of God working in the conviction and conversion of sinners, and to enter spheres deserving attention at short notice. He was specially fond of preaching the Gospel in the open air or in a tent, and some of the most notable missions he conducted were held in canvas cathedrals.

Tent Campaigns

Notable among these were two series of meetings held in the town of Kilmarnock, the first in 1876, and the other in 1892. On both occasions the interest aroused was remarkable, and the numbers attending gave evidence of a real spiritual awakening.

As these lines are being written news of the Home-call of a brother in far-off Canada comes to hand, and at the end of the notice appears these words: "Saved in the tent at Kilmarnock, under the preaching of Alexander Marshall 52 years ago." The fruits of the second mission have enriched the spiritual life of Ayrshire and the West of Scotland. Not a few of those who are doing a notable work in the spread of the good tidings in these parts were brought to the Lord at that time. A leading brother in one of the Assemblies who has been for many years an ardent soul-winner, wrote to Mrs. Marshall as follows: "It is now thirty-six years since your husband led me as a young man of fifteen years of age to Christ in the town of Kilmarnock."

In the summer of 1891, Mr. Marshall took a tent to Dumfries, and there a remarkable work of grace took place. A feature of the work was the number of young men who came under the influence of the Gospel. It was current at the time that the entire staff of a large drapery warehouse in the town had been saved. Certain it is that a great many were, and later these young men were holding honoured positions in several of the large towns of England and Scotland, and bearing witness for Christ in these positions. One of them was the proprietor of a large drapery warehouse in an English watering place. His wife wrote: "We miss Mr. Marshall's card this New Year. He has kept in touch with us, and sent a card yearly since my husband was saved in Dumfries 37 years ago."

In the summer of 1895, Mr. Marshall went to Manchester to take up tent work in Ardwick Green.

The meetings were continued for ten weeks, and the tent could not accommodate all who came. From the first meeting there were evidences of blessing, and by the time the meetings were finished the converts were so numerous that the hall in Water Street was much too small to hold all who desired to come. Hope Hall, in Ardwick Green, is the direct result of these meetings. Now children of the converts, and children's children, are busily engaged in the good work in Manchester; while the ranks of the missionaries in India and China have also had their number increased as an outcome.

One of Mr. Marshall's greatest missions was in Leeds, where he laboured in conjunction with Charles Morton, John Brunton, and, we believe, Rice T. Hopkins. Theatres were hired, and great crowds attracted. CHAS. A. AITCHISON spent hundreds of pounds on this mission, and will share in the Recompense at that Day.

An amusing incident occurred in this connection. Mr. Aitchison, wanting a plain wooden box to hold the hymn books, bought one for 1/6 in the market place. Mr. Morton thought he would do likewise. Going the next day, the stall woman demanded 2/. "A friend of mine got one yesterday for 1/6," said Mr. Morton. "No, no," said the stall-keeper. "Yes," said Mr. Morton, "an old man came down and got one for 1/6." "Oh," said the woman, "yon poor old man! Do you think I could find it in my heart to charge him 2/-? Yes, *he* got one for 1/6, but *you* pay 2/-." And pay 2/- he did.

The "old man" who spent hundreds on the mission, and left £150,000 for mission work, humbly and plainly dressed, got one for 1/6. The preacher, much better dressed, paid 2/-.

Other tent campaigns were held at various times during the fourteen years that elapsed between his return to Britain and the date we speak of, but the places mentioned were landmarks in a most fruitful Gospel ministry.

An Arduous Year

To obtain some indication of Mr. Marshall's industry we have examined a number of his diaries, and find therein records of visits to many places, and prolonged series of meetings often numbering thirteen in one year. The year 1895 was such a year. In the early months of the year he was in Cardiff, Bristol, and Blackburn. In Manchester during April, in Norwich and Carlisle during May. Holding forth in the Royal Spa Concert Rooms in Harrogate during June. Back in the tent in Manchester from July to September. Thereafter in Barrow-in-Furness and Ayr, finishing the year in Glasgow.

The Glasgow work that winter was of a special character. United services were arranged in the East End and in the North-West part of the City. Mr. Marshall preached in the Mechanics' Institute, in Bridgeton, and Mr. David Rea, the well-known Irish evangelist, held forth in Garscube Hall, Garscube Road. Meetings were large, the saints were united and enthusiastic, and the power of the Lord was present to heal. On the Sunday evenings, late meetings, often numbering 1,000 to 2,000, were held in the Olympia, a huge covered-in showground at the top of the Cowcaddens, and there amidst the caravans and trumperies of the show folks, often accompanied by the barking of dogs and other discordant noises, men and women heard the message of redeeming love. He who has declared, "My Word shall not return unto Me void" (Isa 55:11) took care of the seed sown, and saw to its resurrection in the hearts of not a few.

Caring for the Saints

In these days many companies of Christians, the fruit of a period of blessing extending for many years, were seeking to know the will of God as to the principles of gathering, baptism, the Lord's Supper, and kindred subjects. Many of them are now large and prosperous Assemblies, but they owe much to the help received from Mr. Marshall in the days of their weakness. He never taught saints without preaching the Gospel, and it follows, if the believers were being helped, the blessing also reached out to sinners.

In a carefully kept notebook, dates and place-names and subjects spoken on, are recorded, the record going back for nearly thirty years; but in none of his diaries or note books is any record preserved of the numbers who professed faith under his ministry. He had a great aversion to the counting of heads or numbering of the converts. When mention was made that so many had been saved at a certain place, he was quick to correct the statement with the single word "professed," and to quote Donald Ross, who was wont to remark: "Wait till the Books are opened."

It would be an unnecessary task to go into details of special services conducted in many of the large cities of Great Britain over many years. Most of them were of an ordinary character, and in many the experience of former missions was repeated. As Mr. Marshall never followed popular and sensational methods, the repetition of the story, which seems so commonplace in cold type, but was exceedingly thrilling to the actors therein, would prove tedious. Each mission was not equally successful, and sometimes the evangelist and those who wrought with him "toiled and caught nothing;" but success or (apparent) failure were received by him with thanksgiving and without complaint. Whatever he may have thought of the obstacles in the way, and of the low spiritual condition of the believers which prevented the outflow of blessing, he had implicit faith in the Gospel preached, and the simple trust of a little child in God his Father. He never forgot that the grace which grants and the grace which denies came equally from Him.

A Time of Testing

Unfortunately the simplicity which characterised the beginning of what was truly a work of the Holy Spirit was gradually obscured. The unity which is in Christ and which includes all true believers; the fact that the relation of each believer to the Lord and his mutual responsibility to Him and to each member of the Body of Christ were the only ties which bound saints together; that each company of Christians was responsible to the Lord alone; that life and not light was the ground of fellowship; that each member of the family of God was entitled to all the privileges of believers; and that nothing should cut that believer off from fellowship with his brethren save that which cuts him off from fellowship with God. These were the principles which were being put aside, for a recognised fellowship, a circle of Assemblies, and for a sort of presbytery called a district oversight.

Under a plea of preserving the purity of the testimony, these latter things were advocated with a semblance of spirituality and so much vigour, that for a time Mr. Marshall and others, not discerning where this teaching would lead, gave it their support. There came a point, however, when the real sectarian character of this new teaching was manifest, and with it the parting of the ways. That brethren in Christ who had laboured and suffered together should thus separate was a cause of deep heart-searching, but the differences between them concerning fellowship seemed fundamental and irreconcilable, and the "Needed Truth" division took place. This was one of the darkest chapters in the history of the so-called Open Brethren, and one from which the movement has never fully recovered.

Mr. Marshall, Mr. Caldwell, and others did what they could to save the situation, and to their efforts and that of many others may be attributed the fact that the new movement did not receive the support or the following which its leaders expected.

A Breakdown in Health

To men of kindly spirit and sensitive mind like Mr. Marshall, the experience was a great ordeal, and this, combined with many years of arduous evangelising, had its effect on his otherwise robust constitution. In 1896 insomnia began to prove so troublesome as to seriously undermine his health. The nervous exhaustion which was the cause of the trouble proved much more serious than earlier symptoms seemed to indicate, and after intermittent periods of service and suffering, his medical advisers informed him that nothing but a long period of cessation from preaching and complete rest could restore the worn nerve tissues.

Acting on the advice of his doctor he took a trip to New Zealand, and benefited by the voyage. After a stay in that country, lasting over a year, the complaint had not yielded to treatment. Still following the quest for health, he sailed from Auckland to San Francisco, and spent some time in a famous sanatorium in California, but as the benefits were only partial, it was decided he should continue to rest in quietness and away from all excitement. To accomplish this he spent a summer living in a tent among the bush on the shores of Lake Muskoko, in Canada. Progress was very slow, and it was only after he returned to Scotland and settled in Prestwick, in the year 1903, that the distressing ailment began to pass away. Indeed, he never fully cast it off, and undue excitement or overwork brought on recurring attacks of sleeplessness.

From this time onward Mr. Marshall was not able to stand the strain of prolonged campaigns, but for twenty-three years he continued active in the public ministry of the Gospel. Indeed, some of the most steadfast work he accomplished was undertaken in the latter part of his life. His missions were shortened, but his sympathies and activities increased. He knew not how to rest on past achievements, nor did he consult his own ease or comfort. His untiring energy demanded constant employment in the service of the King.

A choice gem of poetry, often used by our brother, best describes the underlying passion which marked his ministry:

"Love strong as death, nay, stronger;
    Love mightier than the grave,
Broad as the earth, and longer
    Than ocean's widest wave.
This is the love that sought us,
This is the love that bought us,
This is the love that brought us
To gladdest day from saddest night;
From deepest shame to glory bright;
From depths of death to life's fair height;
From darkness to the joy of light."

CHAPTER VI

Fulfilling His Ministry

"In journeyings often" was the Apostle Paul's description of his travels in Asia Minor and in Southern Europe. The same words aptly describe the itineraries of Alexander Marshall. Two things combined to keep him continually on the move for many years. His quest for health, and the continual urge of the gospeller's spirit within him. He bemoaned the fact that so few young men had the desire to reach out into needy districts at home and abroad, and he did all he could, not only to stir up interest, but also to supply the lack.

His sympathies were bounded neither by country nor continent, nor by the colour of the inhabitants therein. Every man was a sinner needing a Saviour. Every man could be saved if reached by the Gospel. These two articles in his creed moulded his thought and gave colour to all his actions. Each fresh excursion into new places only served him to reach others with the good news.

An able correspondent and a graphically descriptive writer, many records of these journeys have been preserved. Delightfully interesting pen pictures of the places visited are given, but the background is ever filled with what was the mastering influence of his being. Each fresh scene was looked upon from the standpoint of Gospel opportunity. Even when in enfeebled health, the latent smouldering fire burns in the letters he addresses to friends.

Visits to America

He crossed the Atlantic Ocean on visits to Canada and the United States no less than 36 times, and there were few phases of evangelistic effort on the American continent with which he was not in touch. In New York he was a frequent and always acceptable speaker at Fulton Street Prayer Meeting. He preached the Gospel to the business men and merchants of that city on numerous occasions, and he told the same story to the prisoners in Sing Sing Prison. He enjoye. the friendship of most of the leading Christians in New York, and maintained a regular correspondence with many of them. While he was always faithful to the principles of the New Testament as he had apprehended them, he had a great affection for all saints, and sought to cultivate fellowship with them as far as it was possible to do so.

The same was true of Christians in Chicago, Detroit, and other American cities which he visited from time to time. Few names of accredited and leading Christian workers inside or outside of the Assemblies could be mentioned but Mr. Marshall knew them, and could tell something of their history or their work, quite often adding after this information: "He was saved at one of my meetings."

A Tour in Iceland

In addition to his American tours, he travelled

widely in other lands. In 1897, accompanied by two brethren, R.L. Lundin-Brown, Glasgow, and David Robertson, Galston, he spent fully a month in Iceland, during which time these brethren visited practically the whole island. As there was then no simple Gospel testimony in the island, there is little doubt that the good seed scattered by means of the printed page prepared the way for the more permanent work done by Mr. Arthur Gook and others.

Describing the journey, Mr. Marshall says:

"Through the Lord's goodness we were provided with over 30,000 books, booklets, tracts, leaflets, and illuminated text cards in Danish and Icelandic.

"During our voyage around Iceland, occupying seventeen days, we visited close on thirty ports. On our approach to any place where the vessel was to stay, numbers of boats would put off to us, and on the anchor being cast, the occupants would at once clamber up the ladder and board the steamer. After supplying the visitors with Gospel literature, we usually went ashore and visited the stores and houses, occasionally taking ponies and riding to outlying districts.

"With scarcely an exception, our 'ammunition' was most courteously and thankfully accepted. Priests and peasants, fishermen and farmers, store-keepers and whalers, lads and lasses, crowded around us desirous of obtaining some of the Englishmen's (!) papers. On being supplied they expressed their gratitude by the word 'tak' (which is not the same as the Scottish word with the same pronunciation), or 'thanks.' In many cases the 'tak' was supplemented by a vigorous and hearty shake of the hand. We were inclined to think that tract distribution is not much practised in Iceland. Some of our fellow-passengers took parcels of Gospel literature with them, promising to give them to those who live in their districts.

A gentleman who is a partner in a large business at Vopnafjiord, asked for a quantity of Icelandic, Danish, and French booklets and tracts, telling us that he would undertake to see that they were distributed among the Norwegian, Danish, Faroese, French, and Icelandic fishermen who frequent that part of the coast.

"At an eastern town we visited a steamer which had 200 Icelandic fishermen from the south coast, and were privileged to give them a considerable quantity of booklets, and at Siglafjiord, twenty miles south of the Arctic circle, we came across a whaling fleet with three large blue whales (dead), one of which measured eighty feet. We boarded one of the steamers, and were cordially received by the men. We visited all the 'whalers,' and the hardy fellows seemed pleased at being supplied with our winged messengers. May the harpoon of the Word penetrate their hearts, and may they not be able to extract it until they are safely 'landed!' The weather during the most of our voyage was unusually wet and cold, but on reaching the west coast it became clearer and warmer, enabling us to see the sun shining at midnight.

"On returning to Reykjavik, on Lord's Day morning, 27th June, we received a letter from Dr. Grenfell, Superintendent of the Royal National

Mission to Deepsea Fishermen, inviting us to have an English service on board his mission ship. We were pleased to accept the Doctor's invitation and have fellowship with him and his Christian skipper and crew. After a profitable Bible reading, followed later on by a time of prayer, we had a large Gospel meeting at the corner of a street in Reykjavik. Dr. Grenfell and his skipper, Mr. Lundin-Brown, Mr. Robertson, and myself, in addition to several Danes and Icelanders, took part. We were enabled that night to distribute a large quantity of books and illustrated leaflets."

In Bible Lands

A visit to Egypt and Palestine in 1898 gave him an opportunity to get the rest and restoration his worn nerves so needed, but it also provided him with the means of carrying the message of salvation to practically every place at which the steamer touched. Descriptive paragraphs of Cairo and the Pyramids or of the Jews' Wailing Place are interspersed with stories like the following:

"Some years ago an English lady sojourning in Alexandria besought the Lord to raise up seven young men to preach Christ to the Mohammedans. After waiting on God, six Englishmen, an Irishman, and a Scotsman gave themselves to the work. We were privileged to have a Bible reading with four of these brethren in their house in Alexandria, where they are studying Arabic; also the opportunity of preaching the Gospel in the Soldiers' and Sailors' Home."

In Central America

In 1899, Mr. Marshall visited Central America, calling at St. Thomas, where he had the opportunity of doing some tract distribution among the coloured population. The steamer also made calls at Colon, in the republic of Colombia, and at Greytown, Nicaragua. Opportunities at these ports were limited, but a Government decision made shortly before his arrival gave the servant of Christ good cheer.

These Republics were closed against the Scriptures. The priests had called for Government assistance to prohibit the entry of the Word of God into the country on the ground that it was an evil book. After a prolonged legal argument the Government went against the Church, and decided that the Scriptures should not be excluded.

This cruise ended at Santa Cruz, MEXICO, and here Mr. Marshall had the privilege of spending a few days in the company of Mr. Eglon Harris. This enabled him to see something of the pioneer work which Mr. Harris carried on amidst much persecution, and many obstacles, for many years. Mr. Harris edited and circulated among Spanish-speaking people in Central and South America, a monthly Gospel paper similar in character to *The Herald of Salvation*. He translated and used many of Mr. Marshall's articles in this paper. As the two had so much in common, they were able to rejoice together.

A Sojourn in New Zealand

From a long letter dated 1902 telling of his sojourn in NEW ZEALAND we give one or two extracts:

"At Wanganui we saw a good deal of the veteran evangelist and teacher, Mr. Gordon Forlong. Through his ministry I was brought to Christ in Glasgow in the winter of 1865. Though in his 83rd year, he seems full of life and energy. By pen and voice he preaches and teaches the truth, and contends earnestly for the faith. It was most refreshing to hear him tell the story of his conversion, and of God's wonder-working power in Scotland and England in bygone days. All his large family are saved, and one of his sons is a trader-missionary in the New Hebrides.

"During the past twenty-five years God has richly blessed the labours of His servants in New Zealand. Within that time hundreds, if not thousands, of souls have been saved, and over 100 Assemblies of believers gather simply in His precious Name. For its population, New Zealand is better supplied with evangelists than any other English-speaking country I know of. There are less than 800,000 souls in the whole colony, and it is capable of sustaining ten millions."

The countries in question have greatly developed since these lines were written, but they still give a fair indication of conditions as they exist to-day.

Another long interesting letter in which he gives a vivid description of ports of call between Auckland and San Francisco, and of the ramifications of American heresies in these parts, is closed with the following:

"Surely we have much to learn from others! Perhaps God has a controversy with us as He had with Israel. Maybe one of the reasons why we see comparatively few conversions of late years is because we are not honouring God with our substance. It would do us good to ponder God's message to Israel in Malachi's day: 'Bring ye all the tithes into the storehouse, that there may be meat in My house, and prove Me now herewith saith the Lord of hosts, if I will not open you the windows of Heaven, and pour you out a blessing that there shall not be room enough to receive it' (Mal. 3:7-10).

"If a Jew gave a tithe of his income to God, a Christian surely ought not to be behind him. If even that amount were given to the Lord, there would be plenty of money to spread the Gospel in the regions around and beyond. Because of our unfaithfulness, Mormons and others have got ahead of us, and are sowing tares instead of wheat. 'Give, and you won't feel it,' was the advice once given to a believer. 'Give until you do feel it' replied another. When God's dear people give to Him proportionately, systematic-ally, and bountifully, there will be much more enthusiasm and heart in spreading the glorious Gospel of His matchless grace."

Every work of grace drew out Mr. Marshall's sympathies, and

The Notable Welsh Revival

of 1905 made to him a special appeal. His

observations made after a visit to the scene of the remarkable manifestation proved to be correct. They were as follows:

"During my three weeks' sojourn in South Wales I was privileged to see something of God's wonder working power in the marvellous 'Revival' movement that is going on in the Principality. I visited a number of towns and villages, and had conversations with ministers, evangelists, and Christian workers, and found all were agreed that the movement, in spite of certain excrescences, was of God.

"God has indeed been visiting His people, reviving, refreshing, and restoring them. He has also marvellously blessed the perishing, saving hundreds and thousands of them from everlasting woe. According to the Cardiff *Daily News*, over 70,000 have professed during the past three months in North and South Wales. Statistics of such matters are, however, most unreliable.

"We may as well count the blossoms on the apple tree as fruit as reckon that all who profess to be saved at 'Revival' or 'Gospel' meetings are truly 'born again.' Wherever there is a good threshing of wheat there will doubtless be a considerable amount of chaff. The fields that have been ploughed the deepest, and in which most Gospel seed has been sown, will doubtless produce the richest harvests.

"It seems to be generally believed that the work in Wales originated and has been carried on principally through the labours of Mr. Evan Roberts. This, however, is not the case. There is really no central figure in the movement. In places far removed from each other where Mr. Roberts has never been, and where no special evangelistic efforts have been put forth, the blessing has been abundant.

"A peculiarity of the Welsh work is that, apart from special Gospel preaching, many have professed conversion. A clergyman's recent testimony was as follows: 'The "fire" continues to burn. There have been no sermons in our church for two months.'

"Mr. Roberts' meetings are largely attended. I heard him several times. He speaks quietly and conversationally, and is often so overcome by emotion that he stops and sobs. He appears to be a simple, humble, and whole-hearted follower of Christ. He considers that his special work is to stir up Christians, and seldom remains more than a day or two in a place. The meetings are 'open,' the 'minister,' deacon, elder, choir, organ, and collection (!) being dispensed with.

"It is well to remember that though Mr. Roberts was a church member and 'Christian worker' for years, he has only recently become a Christian. The dear fellow needs our sympathy and prayers, for it is to be feared that he is attempting to do more than he is able. Though there are regrettable incidents in this as well as in all other religious upheavals, we must give thanks to God for what He has done. God's work is perfect, but the moment that man touches it, it ceases to be so.

"One has well said: 'The cynic has scoffed, the critic has sneered, but God has wrought.' 'By their fruits ye shall know them,' is a Divine principle. The Revival movement in Wales, judged by the Lord's words, will stand the test. Sceptics, agnostics, and atheists have abandoned their infidelity and become new creatures. Men who were once drunkards, swearers, gamblers, and prize-fighters are now humble disciples of Christ. Public houses are emptied; churches, chapels, and halls are filled with happy men and women."

The work of the Holy Spirit was not confined to Wales. About this time Quintin Ashlyn, a well-known Society Entertainer, was saved, and thrilled an audience in a London place of entertainment by informing them from the stage that he was unable to give his usual performance, as he had been converted.

By counsel, by literature, and by personal influence A.M. was able to render much spiritual help to this able and courageous young Christian. Interesting letters preserved tell, among other things, that the proprietor allowed the young convert the use of the hall, until he saw the latter's testimony was likely to ruin his business.

CHAPTER VII

Into Regions Beyond

For many years an encouraging Gospel work has been carried on in the WEST INDIES and in BRITISH GUIANA among the coloured people, many of them the descendants of the slaves, and the European settlers. As English is spoken by all, the language presents no difficulty, though at certain seasons the climate is trying.

In response to frequent invitations, Mr. Marshall went there in 1909. His observations and comments included the following descriptive paragraphs:

"The pioneer of the work was Mr. Leonard Strong, a Church of England clergyman, who laboured most assiduously among the white and coloured people in the early thirties. The planters, however, strongly resented his 'interference' with their 'goods and chattels,' placing obstacles in his way to prevent him from ministering Christ to the oppressed and downtrodden slaves. Eventually he withdrew from the English Church, renouncing a salary of £800 a year, in order to be a free servant of the Lord Jesus. God encouraged His ambassador in the path of faith and obedience, showing him the blessedness of depending on Him alone for instructions and supplies. Mr. Strong's ministry was much owned of the Lord. Other labourers were raised up to spread the truth."

Of the voyage to Jamaica and of subsequent happenings he writes:

"Through the kindness of Mr. Maury, one of the editors of the *New York Herald*, I had a letter of introduction to the captain of the 'Orinoco,' whom I found to be a sincere Christian. On learning of my desire to have a Gospel service on the Sunday evening, he gave permission, and helped by asking the boatswain and as many of the crew as he could collect, to attend. I had opportunities of distributing quantities of Gospels and Gospel booklets.

"A good many of the passengers were on their way to Colon and Panama, where 30,000 persons are employed in the construction of the canal. Amongst these were thirty-five persons rescued from the steamer 'Finance,' which was struck and sunk by the 'Georgic' during a fog, off New York, three days previous to our sailing.

"We arrived at Kingston on Thursday, at 10 a.m. We had scarcely reached port when I was asked by a lady if my name was Marshall. The inquirer was Miss Rose Johnstone, an English woman, who speaks fourteen languages, and labours in the canal zone. She had been instructed by a well-known Christian worker to invite me to speak at a meeting in Port Maria, fifty miles distant, that evening. After passing the Customs, and seeing a little of Kingston, I took the train to Albany, forty-two miles north-east, and then drove the remaining eight miles to the place of the meeting. There were 350 men present, mostly coloured, who appeared deeply interested in the proclamation of the 'glad and glorious Gospel.' Five or six remained for conversation.

"During my fifteen days' stay in Jamaica I had ample opportunities of witnessing for the Lord Jesus Christ. At Port Antonia, eighty miles from the capital, the Town Hall was taken for Gospel meetings. On Sunday afternoon the building was crowded. There were 'signs following' these meetings. I spent a week in Kingston, being entertained by an earnest and devoted Christian, who showed us no little kindness."

The description of the period spent in Barbados is both instructive and inspiring.

"Leaving Kingston, we sailed for Colon, the Atlantic port on the Isthmus of Panama, 650 miles distant. Two days were spent there discharging and taking cargo. Eight years previously I visited the city on my way to Colombia; now it is part of the new Republic of Panama. Great changes have taken place since the United States undertook the construction of the canal. Five miles of land each side of the waterway have been purchased by the Americans, and it is called 'The Zone.'

"There is a new town adjoining Colon, called Cristobal, with handsome houses and stores. I took the train to Panama City, a distance of 48 miles, and spent a few hours with an earnest Christian lady who labours among the coloured population of Panama City. The railway track runs along the canal route, crossing the famous Chagres River, which has made the canal so difficult to build. Between 30,000 and 40,000 persons are employed, representing many nationalities and races. Houses, offices, stores, shops and hospitals are erected all along the line. Colon is a most important commercial city, and would make a grand centre for work among Spanish-speaking people. Natives of Colombia, Ecuador, Puerto Rica, Nicaragua, Cuba, and Venezuela throng its streets. There are also thousands from Jamaica, Barbados, and Trinidad.

"Leaving Colon, we skirted the 'Spanish Main, spending a day at Carthagena, an ancient Colombian city, thence to Savanilla, or Port of Colombia. A day was spent at Port of Spain, the capital of Trinidad. Trinidad is one of the most important of the British possessions in the West Indies, yet there is no Scriptural Assembly of believers in the island. Ninety thousand of the population are East Indian coolies, who work on the cocoa, sugar, and coffee estates.

"Ten days after leaving Kingston we anchored in Carlisle Bay, Barbados. During my four weeks' stay in the island I was the guest of Mr. and Mrs. Sparrow at the mission house. Less than six years ago Mr. Sparrow began work in Bridgetown. God gave blessing with the Word, souls were saved and led on in the truth. To-day a company of believers, numbering eighty to ninety, meet in the Gospel Hall for worship and service. Mr. and Mrs. Curtis are doing a good work in the Barbadian capital. A devoted sister, Miss Gallop, had been toiling among her own sex in Dayrell's Road, with considerable blessing. Mr. and Mrs. Sparrow joined forces, and God has graciously given much encouragement. Numbers have been brought from darkness into light, and have been led on in the truth. Bible classes were formed, and the work is steadily growing. A beautiful hall and mission house have been built, with two class-rooms attached. The attendance has so increased that the class-rooms will have to be enlarged. There is a flourishing Sunday school with a staff of earnest teachers. The Assembly now numbers about 120.

He writes of British Guiana: "Mr. W.W. Nichols, who visits the district every three months, invited Mr. John Sparrow, Mr. H.W. Case, and myself to accompany him on one of his itineraries. We left Anna Regina on Tuesday at 7 a.m., in the missionary boat, the 'Messenger,' accompanied by six Christian boatmen, who paddled through 'navigation trenches,' separating sugar estates, across Tapacuma Lake, up the Tapacuma 'creek,' or river, reaching the Government Rest House (which is at the disposal of missionaries) at Pickersgill, on the Pomeroon, a little before sunset.

"Had a Gospel meeting same night, at which several Government officials were present. Next morning we were up early, reaching Lillydale, a settlement of half a dozen houses, at 4 p.m. All of us put up at the mission house adjoining the meeting room. A service had been announced at 7 p.m., and the building was quite full. Hundreds of persons came from various parts of the Pomeroon in their 'corials' and 'batteaux.' Each morning of our stay there was a Bible reading, which was greatly appreciated by the simple, warm-hearted sons of Africa. The evening meetings were crowded with eager and attentive listeners. How I wished we had such appreciative congregations in the 'Old Country,' Canada, or the United States.

"Our time was well spent dealing with 'anxious inquirers.' Lord's Day was a never-to-be-forgotten day by the believers of the Pomeroon. There were morning Bible reading, breaking of bread, and afternoon and evening Gospel meetings. The hall was taxed to its utmost capacity. Early on the Monday morning, with the hearty good wishes, prayers, and benedictions of many, the 'Messenger,' with her passengers and crew, started on her return journey to the coast. Pickersgill was not reached until after sunset. As we left next morning the baboons in the woods gave us a valedictory.

"At Lake Tapacuma we rested and visited an Indian school. In the course of conversation we discovered that the teacher was much interested in God's way of salvation. Anna Regina was reached shortly after sunset. Mr. Nichols took Mr. Sparrow and Mr. Case with him to the mission house at Queenstown, and I became the guest of Mr. and Mrs. C.G. Smith, at Henrietta. The same evening I addressed a meeting in the Gospel Hall. Had three meetings at Henrietta and one at Danielstown, four miles distant. In each of these places there is a small Assembly of believers. Mr. and Mrs. Smith are doing a good work. The hall at Henrietta was crowded, and some appeared to find peace.

"The Danielstown Assembly has been in existence for over half a century, but the Henrietta 'gathering' is only about eight years old. Mr. Smith hails from Kensington Assembly, London, where he was a diligent and active worker for years. The experience he gained during his stay at the Livingtone Medical College has proved of immense service to him in his labours among the East Indians and coloured people. Through being able and willing to help them in their aches and pains he has gained access to their hearts and homes.

"Left Henrietta on the Saturday for Queenstown in charge of Mr. W.W. Nichols, who has 'held the fort' in that important and populous village for over nine years. The work has prospered exceedingly. I enjoyed the meetings I was privileged to have at Queenstown. On Sunday, Monday, and Tuesday we had Gospel services. The meetings were well attended, and there were 'signs following' the preaching of the Word. On Wednesday left Queenstown for Suddie, taking the steamer for Georgetown, which was reached at sundown. A farewell meeting had been arranged for me that night, at which Mr. Wales and I spoke. On the following day I sailed for Barbados, arriving at Bridgetown on Saturday morning, after a somewhat stormy voyage.

"British Guiana is a splendid field for Gospel work, there being an open ear on the part of the people. Whilst evangelists who are willing to endure hardness as good soldiers of Christ are greatly needed, so are men of experience who have the pastor's heart and gift."

A Visit to Russia

In view of the great unpheaval which has taken

place in Russia, and the uncertainty which still exists concerning that vast country, the details of a visit paid to St. Petersburg, in 1910, are of great interest. The titled lady to whom reference is made was Princess Lieven, who died of starvation following the second revolution.

"I was met at the station and had a cordial welcome from Mr. Ivan Prokhanoff, whose guest I am. The Russian capital is a beautiful city, having a population of 1,500,000 souls. Its wide streets and massive buildings, churches and cathedrals, hosts of policemen and military men, attract the attention of strangers.

"God has wrought wondrously during the last few years in opening doors for the proclamation of the Gospel. The Greek Orthodox Church, the State Church of the Empire, is in many respects similar to the Church of Rome. And Rome is essentially intolerant. All along the principal streets are 'ikons,' pictures of saints, with lit lamps and money boxes in close proximity. On the Nevsky, the Regent Street of St. Petersburg, there are shrines in which there are pictures—ikons—of the Madonna and saints. The place is often full of well-dressed people. They cross themselves, kneel, kiss the glass of the picture, and depart. Numbers of people in passing the building cross themselves and hurry on to their work.

"In former days to persuade any one to leave the State Church was to incur a penalty of banishment to Siberia or the Caucasus. A brother who has interpreted for me several times had been sentenced to lifelong banishment to Siberia on two charges:

(1) Breaking an 'ikon,' which cost him 100 roubles (£10); (2) 'perverting' 48 persons! But he escaped to the United States of America, and graduated at the University of Chicago. One who spoke at a meeting with me the other night was banished to the Caucasas for a term of years. The father of my host was also banished, and the son was sought after, but succeeded in making his escape to Finland, a Baron concealing him in his castle. Eventually he reached the friendly shores of England and found a safe retreat.

"At the present time there is liberty for 'Non-conformists' to preach the Gospel in meeting-rooms and buildings that are recognised by the authorities. In St. Petersburg there are ten or eleven halls in which the Gospel of Christ is proclaimed. This liberty is not confined to St. Petersburg. All over the Russian Empire Christians are availing themselves of the opportunity afforded them of telling out the wondrous story of redeeming love. The crowds that attended the meetings held by Mr. Fettler in Moscow, the ancient capital of Russia, caused the church authorities great alarm. Eventually they closed the hall, but, I am glad to say, it is reopened, and the work progresses.

"I have been preaching nightly since my arrival. Seldom, if ever, have I seen such interested congregations. The halls are full, often crowded, on week nights as well as Sunday, with men and women who sit, or stand for hours, listening with rapt attention to the proclamation of God's way of salvation. Our meetings last Lord's Day were as follows: Breaking of bread, 10.30 to 12.30; 3.30 to 4, address to Christians; Gospel, 5 to 7; Gospel from 8 to 10 p.m. I was at the hall from 2.30 until 9.25, leaving before a brother had finished his address. The people do not seem restless or wearied. At both Gospel meetings the seats in the hall, a large and well ventilated building, were occupied, numbers standing all the time.

"There are no special 'after meetings,' but many 'anxious inquirers' are spoken to. On the Lord's Day evening a soldier, about 24 years old, went to the brother who spoke after me and inquired how he could obtain deliverance from the power of sin. A thoughtful and intelligent-looking student appeared greatly troubled about his soul, and was dealt with by one of the brethren. When it is remembered that, until recently, most of the congregations were staunch members of the Greek Orthodox Church, one cannot but feel thankful to God for what He has done.

"The dear people are amazed at what they see and hear in the Gospel halls. They have been accustomed to the ikons and holy water, and genuflections, and they see texts of Holy Scripture and hear that Christ did everything that was necessary for their deliverance, and by believing on the Son of God, who loved them and gave Himself for them, they obtain the free, full, and present forgiveness of all their sins. At first, as it was with us all, it appears to them to be 'too good news to be true.' As a rule, as of old, it is the 'common people' who hear the Word, though there are some exceptions. I have spoken in six halls in the city.

"On two occasions I addressed good companies in

a hall built by the widow of a General,

A Court Favourite

with the late Czar. Madame _____ belongs to the Russian nobility, as well as to the Royal Family of Heaven. The hall, which is a beautiful one, is within her grounds, and many have found peace with God there. Her son took the Doukhobours from Russia to the Canadian north-west. I spoke one evening in a hall, used for meetings, in Princess Lieven's mansion on the Moiskai, and on another evening to a company of 40 believers, mechanics, on the river Neva, close to the shipbuilding yards.

"What a field for labour is Russia, an empire that contains one-sixth of the land surface of the globe, with a population of 150 millions. Within its territories are countries which were once Kingdoms and Empires, the vast majority of whose people never heard 'the old, old story' told out in freshness, simplicity, and power. The Vladivostock Railway is about 6000 miles long, and it is all in Russia excepting that part of it which crosses Manchuria.

"Mr. Kargel, who accompanied Dr. Baedeker in some of his long journeys, now resides and labours chiefly in St. Petersburg. He told me that he had recently obtained a permit to visit the Russian prisons. For fifteen years he has been privileged to proclaim Christ and Him crucified to the tens of thousands of Russian prisoners. The door is open now, but who knows how soon it may be closed."

The present attitude of the Soviet Government towards the preaching of the Gospel is an evidence of how the unlooked for happens, and how quickly great privileges can be withdrawn.

The tide of emigration

To Western Canada

in the years 1906 to 1910 gave Mr. Marshall much exercise, and he made visits to Western Canada in 1906, in 1911, and in 1914, During one of these visits he had the joy of seeing two sons and two daughters of his host, S.W. Benner of Orillia, profess faith in Christ. As the father had been saved during the first mission at Orillia, it was a very great cheer to see fruit thus multiplied.

This report of the special meetings in Vancouver, in 1914, shows that to the end Mr. Marshall attracted large audiences in Canadian cities, and that in the 40 years which elapsed between his first visit and the latter, there had been great progress made. He writes:

"Commenced a series of Gospel meetings in Vancouver on 4th January. I spent some time in the city in the autumn of 1889 and in the winter of 1890. Its population was then about 30,000, and is now over 100,000. The Word preached was accompanied with the Lord's blessing. A hall was secured. A few of us commenced to break bread. Since then the work has gone on. Several companies of believers meet in the city to remember the Lord in the breaking of bread.

"I had hearty fellowship with the Assembly in Mount Pleasant Hall, corner of Main Street and 6th Avenue. A good many of the Christians there are

Sowers

mark 13 - 4 results.

The Sowers Fitness

not only seed good but sowers. J. del'd to saints
See Peter & postman. "Ye are epistles of Xt." but
I - can not - "Only let m. of life" Erasmus
saying — our words have a weight our lives
give them. If people don't see in our lives
what they hear in our words useless

The Work

To sow seed. General & special ministry
Seed has to be sown ere harvest. Seed & soil
have to be brot in contact. (resurrected)

Time to sow

Eccles X. 1-6 - at all times & places the
General sower. Go & them whenever &c
2 Tim 4 - 2 — Be instant (Je mea Bassa,
why not let them to sent up &c.)
& Eccl XI-4 He that observeth
the wind shall. Opportunities passing

"Bow"

Ps 126 - 5 — They that s. in tears —
one reason we reap so little we shed so
few tears. christ & Paul — a weeping
k. makes a w. people. need a passion
souls.

Facsimile of Outline Address, A.M.

from old country gatherings. The large hall of the Central Mission was secured for the special meetings, and we had large week night and Sunday meetings. The last Sunday night about six hundred crowded the building, some being unable to obtain admission. Quite a number professed conversion."

In 1916, despite the menace of the submarine and the frequency with which steamboats belonging to the Allies carrying passengers were attacked, Mr. Marshall again crossed the Atlantic and spent a considerable time

In the West Indies

and in British Guiana. The ready ear for the Gospel among the coloured inhabitants of the islands has been often remarked on. His visit was well timed, and during a depressing period he was a cheer to the servants of the Lord resident there. The following from Demerara is in large measure typical of what he found in the various spheres visited on the mainland and amongst the islands.

"A delightful work of grace has gone on for many years in connection with the Camp St. Assembly. Many souls have been saved, and numbers of God's people have been edified, encouraged, and strengthened. The Gospel testimony is sustained, Bible Class and Sunday school work are engaged in by Christians with heart and soul. I had two weeks' special Gospel services which were largely attended on week nights as well as Sundays. About fifty professed during the fortnight, most of whom were young men and women.

"I was also privileged to have some good meetings in the Bagotstown Hall (Bagotstown is on the west bank of the Demerara River, four miles from Georgetown). Believers have been meeting in the Lord's Name alone in Bagotstown for eighty years. I visited one of the original company, an ex-slave, 105 years old, a happy, hearty Christian. He spoke with deep emotion of the wondrous blessing that attended the labours of Mr. Leonard Strong, an ex-Church of England clergyman, who was the means of his conversion.

"There are eighty in the Assembly, but it is feeble and weak, and is in sore need of a ministering brother with heart and gift to preach the Gospel and tend believers. The hall is a spacious one, but the mission house is in a very dilapidated condition. Mrs. Swift has laboured and toiled among the women and girls for years in spite of frequent attacks of malarial fever. God has blessed her services, and she is at present in Ontario recuperating.

One-third of the people in British Guiana are natives of India, having gone there on the indenture system to work on the sugar estates. They are industrious and hard working people, and most of them remain in the colony and prosper."

It was Mr. Marshall's intention had health permitted to again visit these islands, but God had other plans. There is little doubt that the present wave of blessing sweeping over Jamaica and other of the West Indian isles is an answer to the prayers of Mr. Marshall, and those like-minded, who,

hindered in bodily presence, have reached the
Indies by way of the Throne of Grace.

A Detroit Campaign

The following from a Detroit newspaper is so
true to life and so sympathetic that it must have a
place in this chapter. This special meeting was
probably held during one of A.M.'s last tours in the
United States:

"In the midst of lively argumentation over pulpit
discussion of public affairs, a widely-known 'old-
fashioned Gospel preacher,' Alexander Marshall, of
Glasgow, has begun a series of special meetings at
Salem Hall, Brooklyn Avenue and Perry Street. On
Sunday evening the white-haired veteran showed
the unaltered rigour of his faith by a sermon on
everlasting punishment. All the seats in the hall
were taken. Despite the 'old-fashioned' character of
the preacher's doctrine, there was a clear majority
of young people in the audience and a striking
majority of men hearers.

"Alexander Marshall has been preaching in
Europe and North America and writing books and
tracts for 50 years. One of his writings, 'God's Way
of Salvation,' has been translated into 18 languages,
and nearly 4,000,000 copies have been distributed.
He preached in Canada 40 years ago, when some of
the present-day prosperous cities were lonely
villages. He is preaching the same message to-day
as in the days of his first pioneering.

"'We hope to see people converted in these
meetings,' said Mr. Marshall, opening his talk on

Sunday evening. 'But none will be unless Christians bring their unconverted friends. If there are none here, there will be none to convert.'

"No Need to Envy

"The white old man, with his look of kindly gravity, with an utterance of Saxon English and a slight Scottish burr, stood on the rostrum. Behind and above him was painted on the wall the question: 'Where will you spend eternity?' and beneath it were the words, 'Christ died for the ungodly.' The walls of the room are hung with framed texts emphasizing the same thought. Thus the texts and the wall inscriptions seemed to reinforce the preacher's message. And there was no reference to any public affairs, and only one allusion to a public man:

" 'If you accept the Saviour, you'll have no need to envy Henry Ford—you'll be millionaires for eternity. I am to speak on the question, "Will a God of love punish any of His creatures for ever'" said Mr. Marshall. 'A man will say, "I don't believe He would." My friends, it does not matter what you think, or I think. All that matters is: What does God in His Word say? You and I know nothing at all of what is beyond Time. I wish to-night merely to give you some sayings of God in His Word, and let the water of His Word wash away your preconceived human notions.'

"The preacher then proceeded with citation of texts, turning the pages of his Bible on the desk. And in the audience, too, there was a rustling of leaves, for the people at Salem Hall bring their Bibles with them, and follow the texts.

"The Crowning Sin

" 'The most important conversation recorded in history is that in which the Lord told Nicodemus, "Ye must be born again." The crowning sin of the sinner is that when God has provided salvation for him, he dies rejecting it. If you die in sin, be sure of this, you'll never forgive youself.'

"Mr. Marshall then read the story of the rich man and Lazarus, of how the rich man 'in Hell lifted up his eyes.'

" 'Some say this is a parable,' said Mr. Marshall. 'It is not. Christ says, "There was a certain rich man," and Christ gives the name of the beggar. This story should dispose of any notion that eventually all the wicked will turn up somehow in Heaven, and it will also dispose of any idea that the wicked will be annihilated.

" 'The Epistle of Jude tells us that even now the inhabitants of Sodom and Gomorrah "are set forth as an example, suffering the vengeance of eternal fire." And in the twentieth chapter of Revelation you have a portrayal of what comes to the Christless dead who are "cast into the lake of fire." And in the picture of the Day of Judgment given in Matthew, you find that the same word "eternal" or "everlasting" is used to tell the fate of those who are condemned to punishment and of those who enter into heavenly life.

" 'These are the words of God. It is true that the

Bible is attacked, but it is like shooting boiled peas at the rock of Gibraltar. My best news to you is that you can accept the easy way of eternal life, and be at peace in mind and soul both now and hereafter.' "

On Gospel Pioneering

The following short exhortation written by our brother during his last visit to Canada, fittingly concludes this chapter:

"During seven months recent gospelising in the province of Ontario, Canada, I have been impressed with two facts. (1) That very few scriptural Assemblies have been 'planted' during the last twenty years in Ontario, a province larger than Germany, and twice as large as Great Britain and Ireland; And (2) that in villages and country districts, where such Assemblies existed, there are at the present time none! It is said that evangelists, instead of entering into fresh territory, and breaking up new ground, go from Assembly to Assembly, remaining a week or two, and then departing to a place where there is another gathering. It is not denied that such visits are helpful and fruitful, but the complaint is that strong, healthy young men don't do more pioneering work.

"As I see things, two classes of labourers are specially needed in Canada: (a) Brethren who will make it their business to help small companies of Christians, with little gift, by remaining sufficiently long among them, to stablish, strengthen, and settle them in the truth. If there is but feeble gift in an Assembly, and labourers do not help them, we need not be surprised if the testimony ceases to exist. There are fewer scriptural Assemblies in Ontario than there were twenty years ago.

"When I commenced work in Ontario, in 1880, forty-four years ago, labourers did not wait for 'calls' or 'invitations' from existing Assemblies. In the winter time we preached in school houses, halls, theatres, and meeting-rooms of all descriptions. In the summer the Gospel was heralded in the open air, in barns and tents in districts where there was no clear Gospel testimony, and many were saved. Converts were instructed in the ways of the Lord, were baptised, and met together for worship and Gospel testimony. During the first two years I was in Canada I baptised about 200 in Northern Ontario, and quite a number of believers assembled simply in the Lord's Name.

"The Need of Gospel Pioneers

"And (b): Young men, wholly yielded to the Lord, with a measure of Gospel gift, and a passion for souls, ought to be encouraged to 'launch out into the deep' (where the big 'fish' are) and preach Christ and Him crucified, where there is no clear Gospel testimony. If brethren were to encourage servants of the Lord who are fitted to do such work in needy and neglected fields—and stand by them—there would be more pioneers.

"Many Assemblies have fellowship with gospellers when they are labouring in their midst, but not at any other time. It is admitted that gospellers should look to the Lord alone for their support and guidance. It is well, however, to remember that the 'best of men are only men at the best,' and if evangelists are invited by Assemblies to preach in their meeting-rooms, and their needs are fully met, whereas the pioneer has a hard struggle to make 'both ends meet,' one is not surprised that in some cases such 'invitations' are accepted, and the 'regions beyond' are neglected. The Lord Jesus is the Head of the body. Let us then at our public meetings, and prayer meetings, plead with Him to raise up more pastors and evangelists. Let us remember the Divine declaration: 'If two of you shall agree on earth as touching anything that they shall ask, it shall be done for them of my Father which is in Heaven' (Matt. 18:19)."

CHAPTER VIII

Personal Gifts

A Christian worker of many years' experience, himself an evangelist, and one who knew Mr. Marshall intimately, frequently said that he believed if a man, sincere in his desire to know the truth, went to hear Alexander Marshall preach, he would not leave the meeting without the assurance of sins forgiven. There is no doubt that Mr. Marshall never addressed a Gospel meeting without putting before his audience the truth in the way a child could understand, which once apprehended brings forgiveness and peace.

It was this quality in his preaching which made him the soul-winner he was. He preached for results, and seldom failed to get them. His messages were packed full of saving truth. Quoting Duncan Mathieson, "he liked to put in the needle of the law threaded with a long thread of grace." His addresses always dealt with vital subjects, the need of the sinner, the sufficiency of the Saviour, and the ground of justification, all had their proper place. Unlike many modern addresses, the appeal was the subordinate thing. "It is the truth believed and received which gives assurance;" "It is not a man's decision, but his belief of the truth, which saves," were two things he never forgot, and two statements he constantly repeated to others.

Plainness of Speech

Reiteration was a marked feature of his preaching. He firmly believed that repetition of a foundation fact or a Gospel statement fixed it on the hearer's mind, and in this way he drove home eternal truths, as the joiner drives home the nail by repeated blows of the hammer. His addresses were also well lighted with windows. Apt illustrations were never wanting to make plain the meaning of a passage or a statement. His remarkable memory for facts and details enabled him to bring from the treasures accumulated during his wide experience a wealth of illustrations and incidents. Arrows of Divine truth we feathered with a telling phrase or a well selected verse, and often found a joint in the harness of the stout rebel against God.

His English was good, and he never failed to use great plainness of speech. His language was the every-day phraseology of the people among whom he served. It was mostly confined to words of two syllables. What he said was charming in its simplicity. He was wont to say: "I endeavour to speak to the ninety-nine per cent," and in this he succeeded as few of his contemporaries did. He cultivated the habit of speaking slowly and distinctly, and used the clear, rich voice with which God had endowed him with wonderful effect. How carefully he used it was evidenced by the fact that at eighty his voice was as clear as a bell, and he could make himself heard to large audiences without effort as long as he was able to preach.

His Favourite Themes

were the outstanding Gospel verses of the New Testament, the parables and miracles of the Lord Jesus, and the striking redemption passages of Isaiah. The remote text and the far-fetched illustration were always to him a cause of irritation. "Why seek a text to put the Gospel into it?" he was wont to say, "when there are so many plain Gospel statements in the Word of God." The ring of conviction and sincerity was present in all he said, and the time-worn phrase or quotation came with freshness from his lips.

To him the Gospel was not something to be proved or to be apologised for, not even something to be explained. It was a message to be preached, and he preached it with no uncertain sound. The scope of his theology is best defined in a favourite epigram of his own: "There is a Christ for every sinner out of Hell, and a Hell for every sinner out of Christ."

An index book which he carefully kept over a period of many years and which contains entries against many towns on the North American Continent, British Guiana, and places in Britain as remote as hamlets in the Hebrides and the Shetland Islands, furnishes information as to the texts and topics from which he preached. Those who knew our brother will not be surprised to learn that the following subjects, "A midnight scene in a prison cell," "Can a man be saved and know it?" "Will a God of Love punish any of His creatures for ever?" and "God's Great Whosoever" (John 3:16) have the premier place in the frequency of their use for Gospel messages, while "Soul-winning" was his most used topic in talks to believers.

He could never be content or satisfied with just

The Ordinary Meeting

nor could he be satisfied with large companies. He never measured an audience by the number present, but by how many of that audience were strangers in the truest sense of the word. Unless the gatherings were mostly composed of sinners he was ill at ease. He was never happy preaching the Gospel to saints or to seats. Like a good fisherman, his desire was to fish in a pond where fish were present. This he did, and God made him a fisher of men.

It is not to be supposed that Mr. Marshall was shallow or superficial, or that his view on life was narrow and restricted. His love for God gave him a big heart, and a wide outlook. One could not spend much time in his company without discovering he was extraordinarily well informed on most subjects. His widely extended travels, coupled with keen powers of observation, and a remarkably retentive memory, furnished him with such a fund of general knowledge as made him an entertaining and instructive companion, the more so because all he had acquired was subjected to the ruling passion of his life.

He was a keen and

Diligent Student of Scripture

and as a theologian was master of the great
foundation doctrines of Christianity. Those who
crossed swords with him either in debate or in
correspondence were soon aware that there were
few of the subtilties of theological argument, for
which a past generation of Scotsmen were famous,
that he was not acquainted with. Yet through it all
there shone the sterling simplicity of his character.
He loved the plain and simple things, consequently
he never founded a doctrine on a tabernacle pin or
cord. He was wont to say: "Why walk in the
rushlight when the sun is shining?" and as to the
teaching of theoretical prophetic subjects, he
invariably answered: "It's a great downcome for an
evangelist to become a prophetic lecturer."

Frugality and carefulness were marked traits in
his complex character, and in spiritual things as well
as in temporal he never allowed anything to waste.
Incidents related to him which might be helpful in
preaching or which might be suitable as an
illustration in a tract were carefully noted and
preserved. Outlines of Bible study and Gospel
addresses were prepared and filed for future use.
His notebooks also contain many gems of poetry,
and epigrams collected from various sources, and
now familiar to his friends through the frequency
with which he used them. Paul's exhortation: "Give
thyself wholly to them," was literally obeyed by Mr.
Marshall in his devotion to the Gospel. His Bibles
contained a number of half sheets of paper with the
outlines of an address noted thereon. These scanty

notes were all he used even for addresses to believers. In his ministry of the Gospel the words came from a heart inditing a good matter, without note or external aid. The threefold cord of ruin, redemption, and regeneration, usually in this order, ever predominated.

As a Personal Worker

A story Mr. Marshall frequently related concerned a lady who during a sea voyage complained that one of her fellow-passengers, a gentleman, had been rude to her. "What did he say to you?" inquired her husband. "He asked me if I was saved," was the reply. "Then you should have sent him about his business," rejoined the husband. "But unfortunately he seemed to be about his business," said the wife. This incident could have been true of the subject of this sketch. To use an old Scots phrase: "He was aye at it."

The Lord who spoke to the multitudes on the side of the lake, waited at the well of Samaria for the woman of the city in order to speak to her the Word of Life. The Spirit who used Philip the evangelist in the revival in Samaria, caught him and sent him to the desert place at Gaza, in order to meet the Eunuch of Ethiopia. The same Lord and the same Spirit made use of Mr. Marshall in the same way, and he was as much at home in dealing with the individual in an inquiry meeting as he was in preaching from the platform. With him there might be a change of method, but there was no change in the message.

In the same way it seemed natural for him to engage his fellow-passengers on train or steamboat in a conversation which led up to a presentation of the Lord Jesus as the Saviour of sinners. Wherever he went he made it his business to speak to all who would listen to him about eternal realities, and only *that day* will declare how many he thus pointed to the Saviour. Not that he was easily satisfied with professions or counted numbers. He delighted to present the simple truth of the Gospel, and allow the Spirit of God to apply it to heart and conscience.

He was the most persistent and

Indefatigable Tract Distributer

I have ever known. Wherever you met him, his pockets bulged with tracts and booklets, and in season and out of season he scattered the good seed. His seed basket was always carefully stocked, and he skilfully presented the Word in season. A brightly coloured picture, a glittering medal, a pocket mirror with a Gospel text on the back, were some of the treasures he unfolded for the bairns, while to the elders the striking text, the pictorial leaflet, or the small booklet were dealt out with the same judicious care.

He carried on his work on the same principle as the Scottish Laird, whose advice to his son was: "Aye be planting a tree, it will be growing while you are sleeping." If all the Lord's people showed the same earnestness and care for the souls of others, the looked-for revival would soon be with us.

Neither in preaching nor in personal dealing was

New Buildings,
Barnstaple,
Devon.
28. Nov. 99

Facsimile of Letter from Mr. R.C. Chapman of Barnstaple

Mr. Marshall's address likely to be soothing. It never would be said of him that he was a preacher who preached a sermon that touched no man's conscience. His presence had a disturbing effect, but if men took the offence it was because they did not know the warm heart behind the message, nor understand the burning passion to make all men see and obey the truth which actuated all he did.

Whatever his attitude may have been in regard to conversion in his early preaching days, he certainly was not easily satisfied during the last thirty years, when he won hundreds for Christ. He took great care as to how the anxious were dealt with in his aftermeetings. If he found anyone saying, "Believe that and you are saved," he would point out the danger of "believing in their believing" instead of "believing in Christ."

An Example and an Appeal

His method of personal dealing is shown by the following incident related by himself:

"I was speaking to a farmer in Northern Ontario, Canada, about the salvation of his soul. He seemed to be exceedingly desirous of learning God's way of salvation. He was looking within to obtain peace. As well might a serpent-bitten Israelite expect to be healed by looking at his wound, as a sinner hope to be saved by looking into his cold, unbelieving heart. Opening my Bible, I slowly read, clause by clause, the familiar and oft-quoted but little understood Isaiah 53:6: 'All we like sheep have gone astray; we have turned every one to his own way; and the Lord hath laid on Him the iniquity of us all.' I sought to get him occupied with Christ and His finished work, reminding him that we are saved through what He did for us, and not through what we do for Him. But he continued occupied with his feelings toward God, instead of with God's feelings toward him.

"Observing a text on the wall, I pointed him to it. It was a most suitable Scripture for the occasion: 'Behold the Lamb of God which taketh away the sin of the world' (John 1:29). The seeking soul lifted his eyes, and gazing intently on it, read it slowly and carefully. Then turning suddenly to me, he exclaimed, 'Glory be to God! I see it now, Jesus has died for me and I am saved.' A Christian who had known him for years said, 'How do you know that you are saved?' The eyes of the young convert sparkled with joy as he replied: 'Jesus has died for me.'"

The following is the final paragraph of an address on soul-winning, which he must have given many times, and in many lands:

"We may plead our ignorance and unfitness to engage in the glorious work of soul-winning. God is able to supply our every need if we are but willing to yield ourselves unreservedly to Him. Let us 'lift up our eyes, and look on the fields, that are white already unto harvest.' These 'fields' lie around us, as well as beyond us. We know the disease of sin and the cure. Thank God, we are assured that the Gospel 'is the power of God unto salvation to every one that believeth" (Rom. 1:16). May the Lord stir us up to feel our personal responsibility to make known to others what Christ's death has accomplished. May we not forget that, whatever is our occupation, our business is, as having been 'put in trust with the Gospel,' to spread it, and make it known to those who are heedless and careless of their truest and best interests."

CHAPTER IX

The Pen of a Ready Writer

Widely as Mr. Marshall travelled, the numerous articles from his facile pen have reached even wider bounds. A.M. tracts have an extensive circulation in every English-speaking country in the world. They are used by evangelical Christians of every denomination, and leaders of evangelistic effort declare there are none better. A great number have found their way into the hands of English-speaking people in European and Asiatic lands, and have been used in the conversion and blessing of not a few.

Mr. Marshall early began to write. Dr. James Morison made use of some of his articles in the publications of the Evangelical Union Church, and from these early days to the end of his long and useful life his pen was never idle. Mention has already been made of his literary efforts in Canada and of the founding of the *Gospel Herald*. At the same time he was a regular contributer to the *Herald of Salvation*, a Gospel periodical published in Glasgow, founded by the late R.T. Hopkins, in 1878, and edited by him for a number of years. In 1893, when Mr. Marshall returned from Canada he was asked by Mr. Pickering to undertake the editorship. From that time until his decease the *Herald of Salvation* was his favourite child. Articles from his pen appear in every issue. A striking incident, a personal conversation, or an inquirer's difficulty, were his favourite starting points, and from these to application and illustration is an easy journey. For a clear and simple presentation of the doctrine of the Cross they are unexcelled.

In addition, he was a frequent contributor to *The Witness*, and a number of serial articles, as "Voices from the Vineyard" and "Leaves from an Evangelist's Note Book," are pleasing and profitable reading.

A Famous Booklet

His most noteworthy contribution to evangelical literature was the little booklet *God's Way of Salvation*, illustrated by comparison and contrast, which is a classic of its kind, and with the possible exception of *Safety, Certainty, and Enjoyment*, has been the most widely circulated Gospel book ever issued. The book deals with the excuses and difficulties which arise when the offer of the Gospel is presented to the sinner. The articles of which it is composed were first issued as two separate booklets, but acting on the advice of the publishers, Mr. Marshall put them together and issued them in their present form. The circulation has nearly reached the five million mark, and from the date of its issue until the present it has been used to the awakening of the careless and the assuring of the anxious in a remarkable way. It has been translated into fourteen different languages, including Spanish, French, German, Italian, Russian, Danish, Dutch, and Egyptian, besides Welsh and Gaelic, and is used by missionaries and evangelists in all parts of the world. Thousands were given to inquirers during the campaigns of Dr. Torrey and C.M. Alexander, and Dr. Chapman and Mr. Alexander.

Thousands who never met the author have received

Blessing from Reading the Book

and hundreds of testimonies have been received from those who have been convicted and converted from its perusal. It is impossible to cite more than one or two, but these read as wonderful as anything which has ever been written concerning evangelical work.

This letter was written by a well-known worker in Australia, in 1924:

"In 1917 I left Australia for England in connection with the war, and was brought in touch a good deal with my uncle and cousin. The former is an elder brother in the Shortlake Assembly, and the latter at the Barnet (formerly Tonbridge and Whetstone) Assembly. I was a Church of England adherent, but unsaved, and had many discussions with my relatives on religious matters, but mainly on prophecies. When leaving for the return journey to Autralia I took a number of tracts and booklets to read on the way, including the one mentioned above and written by you, which was pressed into my hand by my uncle.

"The first evening out from Liverpool, when in the Irish Sea, I was dressed ready for dinner at 6.15 (on 6th January, 1918), and to fill in the time waiting for the gong, started to read *God's Way of Salvation*. Halfway through the Holy Spirit dealt with me, and caused me to cry out from my heart, and I accepted the Lord Jesus Christ and His finished work. As a guilty sinner I came to Him, who alone could save me. Instantly I felt the change in my heart as the Holy Spirit came to me, and I knew that I had passed from death unto life, and felt myself to be literally walking on air for days afterwards.

"At the beginning of this year I felt that the call came for me to undertake individual soul-winning, and I shall never forget the joy I experienced upon leading the first convert to the Lord Jesus Christ—but to Him alone be all the glory. Day by day, week by week, the work is going on, and up to date twenty-two dear souls have been brought to know and love their Lord. It is my constant prayer that God will make me more and more zealous in His service, with a passion for souls, that our dear Lord may be magnified and His love experienced by many who must otherwise perish. The first convert brought her sister to the Lord within a few months, and her mother was saved in my office last month."

The following incident was sent on to Mr. Marshall by the author of this biography a few days after it happened:

"A young man came into my room in the office a few days ago, seeking information regarding the Keswick Convention. During conversation, he informed me he was on a visit to this country from South Africa, preparatory to entering upon missionary service. Relating the story of his conversion, he told of entering his bedroom in his lodgings in Johannesburg on a Sunday evening.

Noticing a little booklet, *God's Way of Salvation*, on the table, he picked it up and read it through. Now interested, he read it a second time, until he came to the portion which begins, 'God says I'm saved.' As he did so the truth flashed in upon his soul, and in the faith of a child he took in the good news."

A Christian worker in Glasgow told us the following striking incident about a sea captain who was saved in India through a Gospel tract. "Captain McM_____ was brought up in a Scottish Christian home, and had the unspeakable privilege of sound instruction in the things of God. Soon after going to sea he ceased reading his Bible, becoming careless and indifferent about eternal concerns. Through reading pernicious literature he was tempted to become an infidel, but the godly example of his parents kept him from openly denying the truth of Christianity. He knew that if the Scriptures were true he deserved eternal banishment from the presence of a holy and sin-hating God.

"One Sunday morning his steamer arrived at Calcutta. After breakfast he went to bed and read for a considerable time. Uneasy in heart and conscience, he began to ponder the following questions: 'Is there a God?' 'If there is a God, where is He?' 'Where are my parents?' 'Are they in the grave or are they in a place of bliss?' Whilst thus engaged, a knock was heard at his cabin door. Unwilling to be disturbed he made no response. A second and louder knock was heard, and he shouted, 'Who's there?' but no one spoke. Observing that the door was being gradually opened, he exclaimed, 'Don't come in here.'

"Through the partially opened door an out-stretched hand holding a Gospel booklet appeared. The captain saw no form, though he could easily tell that the hand was that of a man. The book was accepted, and the 'Lord's messenger' with the 'Lord's message' departed. The captain glanced at the title page of the book, which was *God's Way of Salvation*. As he perused its pages the Holy Spirit convicted him of sin, and revealed to him that his whole life had been one of rebellion against a Holy God. Rising from bed, Captain McM_____ fell on his knees confessing his guilt, and was led to see that Christ by His death on Calvary had settled once and for ever the 'sin question.'

"Great was his joy when he perceived that by believing on the Lord Jesus, who was wounded for his transgressions and bruised for his iniquities, he was pardoned, justified, and saved for eternity.

"Since that

'Happy day that fixed his choice
On Christ his Saviour and his Lord.'

Captain McM_____ loves to tell of his conversion to God through a Gospel booklet given to him in his cabin by an unknown Christian worker in the city of Calcutta. The captain has not been able to ascertain the name of the tract distributor to whom he is so much indebted. The likelihood is that the courageous and diligent tract distributer will not know till he reaches the Glory the result of that Sunday morning's seed sowing."

The story of how a woman was helped out of the

depths by the booklet is given by a Sydney Christian worker:

"Early in 1915 I was labouring in the Gospel in the River Murray district of this State. A woman, who, with her neice, had been running a house of ill-fame, attended one of the meetings. At the end of the meeting she asked that I should visit her. I did so several days later, read from Romans 3, prayed with her, and left a copy of *God's Way of Salvation*. It resulted in her conversion. She posted it to the neice who had married and gone to live elsewhere. She, too, was saved through its perusal."

Altogether nearly four hundred similar stories could be furnished.

A Remarkable Circulation

The circulation of the book also presents some remarkable features. Close on forty years ago a brother in one of the Glasgow Assemblies encouraged three young men to commence posting a copy to addresses which he supplied to them. Thus commenced what is known as Glasgow Gospel Postal Work, which has in the intervening years been greatly enlarged. Numerous bands are at work on various centres, and in this way a great number of *God's Way* has been carried direct into homes which were in measure prepared for the good seed. During the great war the lists of the killed were carefully gone over, and wherever the addresses of bereaved relatives could be found, the mourners received a message of sympathy and a copy of the book.

A professional gentleman resident in Glasgow was so struck with the suitability of the book that he arranged for the distribution of 250,000 copies on the streets in Glasgow, a work which kept an elderly Christian man employed for several months.

A Glasgow business man, the late Mr. C.P. Watson, made a careful plan of the West End of Glasgow, and posted thousands of copies to the homes of the rich and well-to-do people of the city. More recently, Tom Rea, son of David Rea, Irish Evangelist, has posted thousands of copies to addresses in the South and West of Ireland.

As we go to press a gentleman in Australia who was saved through "God's Way" sends £50 to the publishers to help in the free distribution of the book.

In these and many similar ways the saving truth of the Gospel has been scattered. What a harvest will be made manifest in *That Day* when sower and reaper will rejoice together.

In Other Languages

"Reaching farther out" was the motto which the author had before him in connection with his booklet, as in other matters of Christian service. The ever widening circles of influence and usefulness was the reward he coveted.

When the end came he was busily engaged in making arrangements for the translation of *God's Way* into some of the many languages of India. Shortly before his death he completed arrangements with the publishers of the English Edition, by which the rights are theirs. This will secure that the circulation will continue uninterruptedly.

A new and fine translation into Russian has just been completed, and part of this edition has been forwarded to Esthonia. What those Russian and Esthonian friends think of the book is evidenced by the following short note from Adam Podin, a very trustworthy and spiritually minded brother:

"I ordered my son to write you a letter and tell you how much blessing your book, *God's Way of Salvation* (Esthonian Edition) has brought to our land. I preach in the prisons, and give to each prisoner a New Testament and a copy of *God's Way of Salvation*. Several prisoners have been converted . . . I preached the Gospel to the lepers. The book, *God's Way of Salvation* has opened many eyes, and they now see the 'way.' I think this is the best book next to the Bible."

His smaller Gospel booklets: *The Story of My Conversion*, *Twice Rescued from Slavery*, *Saved at Seventy*, and *A Highlander's Conversion*, have had an extensive sale and been blessed to many.

His booklet *God's Wonderful Love*, contains the best of the many stories he told on this—certainly one of his favourite texts.

Another pamphlet which has had an extensive circulation is *Straight Paths for the People of God*. In it the principles of New Testament gathering, fellowship, and reception are set forth in a helpful and instructive fashion.

One missionary in Central Africa had reason to thank God for an earlier booklet, *Wandering Lights*, of which *Straight Paths* was a new edition, as the following will show:

"That book was given me when I was about a year and a half in Central Africa, on Inazinga Hill Station, and clearly led me to see the hollowness of the systems, even in such as the one I was in. In time of depression and trouble, when seeking to know God's will, I would take that book and my Bible and seek its help. Nothing taught me more in all my life's history, about the truth, and I could not express how much I longed to be where it pointed to."

A.M. was the author of numerous pamphlets written in defence of the faith. One of these, *Will a God of Love Punish any of His Creatures for Ever?* is the substance of a favourite address. Its issue and circulation proved timely in view of the growth of "Non Eternity" teaching.

Ever a valiant for the truth, he published numerous trenchant criticisms of modernistic theories. The last of these was, *Christ or the Critics*, an answer to the thinly veiled rationalism which followed the war. A large edition was quickly exhausted, and there is every reason to believe it proved a help to many whose faith was shaken by these strange doctrines.

CHAPTER X

Mr. Marshall's Correspondence

Mr. Marshall had a more than ordinary ability of making and retaining friendships, and in order to do so he conducted an enormous correspondence. The converts of his various missions, leaders of meetings, his hosts and hostesses during his journeys, fellow-evangelists, young workers setting out to reach unevangelised parts, were all kept in touch with by his letters. Generally his letters were not long, but they were sufficient to give his friends a few interesting items regarding the work he was engaged in, the places he visited, and a short word of comfort or encouragement.

He seemed to have a regular list, and in all his journeyings he never forgot to post to these friends a few picture cards with views of the towns or the country he was passing through. Not a few of these form collections in Christian homes, where they are retained and treasured. He never sent out a letter without enclosing with it a suitable message in the form of a tract, leaflet, or card. Sometimes a simple Scripture text, sometimes a few lines of choice poetry, sometimes an extract from an eminent writer's work, but always suited to the need of the person to whom it was despatched.

In addition to this, however, his correspondence with his contemporaries concerned many of the difficulties which have arisen in the carrying on of a

Gospel testimony and a Church order after the pattern of New Testament simplicity. Unfortunately Mr. Marshall's letters have not been preserved, but the historical value of the replies which he has retained are such that it is fitting that one should be included.

The reply is from Mr. ALEXANDER STEWART. It is dated 26th Feb., 1880, and deals with

"Shepherd Care

"To the passages in your letter in which you deprecate controversy with fellow-saints, and say that you mean to stick to the Gospel, I heartily say 'Amen.' Time is too short and energy too precious to be wasted on fruitless contention. Fish for men. It is true, as you say, that we are earnestly to contend for the faith, but that surely does not mean fighting among ourselves.

"This winter I have been taking a meeting regularly on the Wednesday evenings for exposition of Scripture. Last night the subject was the shepherd-care of the Lord Jesus—arrived at in this way: I have been taking up the parables, chiefly in Luke's Gospel, and had been considering that of the good Samaritan. The obvious lesson of course is, mercy to our neighbour, but you are acquainted with the view which sees the wounded man, 'half-dead,' the sinner (whole-dead and yet capable through grace of being brought into life and health), and in the good Samaritan the Saviour of sinners. The parable was thus considered, and having looked at the first Gospel aspect of it—the

Mr. Marshall in the Uniform of the Soldiers'
Christian Association

wounded man delivered—we came to the second, *i.e.*, the saved man brought into the 'inn' and placed under the care of the 'host,' for the period between the going away and coming again of the Samaritan a condition answering to our present state.

"Our sins are forgiven, we are saved in that sense, but are also brought under the care and guidance of the Shepherd and Bishop of our souls during the time that may elapse between our conversion and His return. You will notice that the 'taking care' is the part both of the Samaritan (Luke 10:34) and the host (v.35), answering in the one case to the pastorship of the Lord Himself and in the other to that of the Under-Shepherd whom he raises up to oversee the flock. The word, so far as I know, is used in only one other place in the New Testament Scriptures, 1 Tim. 3. 'How shall he "take care" of the Church of God."

"In connection with this subject, John, chap. 10, was looked at. There the Lord is spoken of as 'the Door of the sheep' and as the 'Good Shepherd.' We come in by Him, and having come in, we are henceforth under His guidance. When we enter we are saved; we go in and out, having liberty (free of the fold, like children of the house), worshipping in the sanctuary, serving in the world, and we find pasture—led into it, as in the 23rd Psalm. This is the happy and peaceful side, but in the 10th of John, as in the 23rd Psalm, there are 'enemies,' and the flock and the shepherd are concerned with them.

"There is need for contention, the point I set out with above. But of whom must the sheep beware, and with whom, on their behalf, must the shepherd contend? In the 10th of John these four are mentioned—the stranger, the hireling, the thief, and the wolf—the last two being positive enemies with evil designs upon the flock. Now would we not do well to test our contentious energy by the question: Is he against whom I contend a stranger, a hireling, a thief or a wolf, or otherwise? Is the doctrine I combat the doctrine of the stranger, hireling, thief, or wolf? Am I seeking to exclude the voice of the stranger and the ministry of the hireling or to prevent the seductive drawing away of the thief and the scattering devouring havoc of the wolf? I think you may see the thief and the wolf in Acts, chap. 20, explained by Matthew 7:15, and certainly there is a call to withstand them as well as to feed the flock, but the latter is the main duty, and combative natures may need to guard against the desire of wolf-hunting for its own sake.

"Your chosen post is at the Door, stick to it. The great thing for sinners is to get them to enter in, and for saints to bring them under the guidance of the great Shepherd of the sheep. Taking this large view, we may be less troubled about the other door-question you allude to in your letter. Let us start with this clearly before the mind—the door of the local church is not the Door of the 10th of John. Nevertheless, the local church has a door, and should have doorkeepers. The great question for them to solve with regard to an application for admission is, Is he a sheep? The 9th of Acts shows that the Damascus believers were satisfied that Paul was one, and let him in. But the Jerusalem ones were not, and kept him out, though he had been taken in at Damascus. Subsequently it appears that on testimony which satisfied them, they became content to let him in.

"There is another question—a true sheep may be a tainted sheep. In the interests of the flock, to take no higher view, he must be kept apart. In one place there may be a handful of the Christians meeting together, true saints, loving and cleaving to the Lord, but without the door-keeping element largely developed, simple souls, not very formal, who readily receive those whom they believe to have the spirit of Christ. In another, you may have a large gathering, not easily satisfied, who have adopted a regular mode of admission. In either case the applicant is received by the Church, and he is received on the faith of testimony, slenderer testimony, it may be, in the one case than the other, but the principle is the same. I do not see much difficulty. In a well ordered Church you will, no doubt, have men who addict themselves to the door. Let them be vigilant, anxious to admit the true as well as to keep out the false, and let the Church which they serve honour and trust them, cordially receiving those whom they commend to its fellowship. It is very much a question of confidence. Where there is spirituality there will be trust, love, and esteem. Apart from spirituality, of what avail are rules?"

CHAPTER XI

The Activities of a Veteran

In spite of advanced years, the call of the late Great War stirred Mr. Marshall to greater endeavour on behalf of the young manhood, the flower of the nations, which was so ruthlessly maimed and slaughtered in the awful carnage. From the first his great desire was to get to France and as near the firing line as possible. Military regulations are hard to overcome, and it was not until 1918 that he was granted the necessary permission to go to the theatre of war under the auspices of the Soldier's Christian Association.

The intervening years had not been fruitless. Besides doing a good work among the troops in training near his home, he had been able to conduct services in some of the large camps in this country, and had also visited the sick and wounded in the hospitals in various parts of Britain, ministering consolation and preaching Christ.

In the Internment Camps

In July, 1915, he went to Holland and spent some time in the internment camps in that country, among the British soldiers and marines who were interned after the capture of Brussels by Germany. During the months he was in Holland he conducted meetings for the 1,500 British Bluejackets in the camp. Many of the men attended the meetings and not a few professed. Apart from the spiritual help he was able to give to many, his visit was a cheer to men whose conditions were depressing in the extreme. No wonder they welcomed the personal conversation he had with some and the spiritual literature he was able to circulate among them.

As a result of a visit to the United States and to the West Indies, in 1916, he got into communication with a number of Christian friends in the United States who were anxious to get a quantity of Gospels and Scripture portions into Russia. Mr. Marshall was commissioned to arrange for this being done, and on his return to Britain in September he paid a visit to Stockholm, in Sweden, where friends arranged for the reception of the Scriptures and their despatch to accredited Christian workers in Petrograd and elsewhere.

In the War Zone

On June 30, 1918, Mr. Marshall left London for Rouen, and arrived at his destination without mishap the following afternoon. Mr. Byrnell, London, the Secretary of the Soldiers' Christian Association, tells of his final interview with him before his departure. Warning him that in these huts where the men were provided with facilities for reading and writing, and such recreations as drafts and dominoes; where they were allowed to smoke and feel as near as possible at home, he might find the atmosphere different from the regular Gospel services to which he was accustomed; that

Mr. Marshall at his Favourite Work

when he commenced to speak a number might rise
and go out; that a man might keep his cap on during
prayer, and that, worst of all, he might find women
preaching in some of the huts; that a wise
forbearance was necessary in the curious circumstances in which the work was carried on. Mr.
Marshall's reply was: "Aye, I suppose so. It's war
time." However, Mr. Byrnell adds, though Mr.
Marshall saw a great many of the things mentioned,
he continued with his work at the Camps and
Railway Station, his haversack filled with books and
tracts for distribution.

He remained at Rouen until August 23rd, a
period of about eight weeks, sharing in the ordinary
work of the hut at the Cavalry Base Depot, getting
into personal contact with the men down from the
firing lines for rest and recuperation, conducting a
Bible Class and preaching the Gospel nightly. A
fortnight was spent at Buschy, then another
fortnight at Rouen, after which he was transferred
to Trouville, where he remained until October 9th.
Thus four of the darkest months of the war were
spent almost within sound of the noise of battle,
and never free from danger and anxiety, but withal
a period of fruitfulness in the service of the Lord.

A letter written from Newcastle, on March 3rd,
1920, by a young man converted at Buschy, is the
story of very many who had similar experiences,
and who shall answer the final roll-call in that Day:

"I was one of the many soldiers, who during a
stay in the camp at Buschy, France, came to know
the Lord Jesus as a personal Saviour. I first heard
you proclaiming the Gospel in a hut at Rouen, and,

frankly, I did not much enjoy that meeting, and kept to my vow not to go back to that hut; so I didn't greatly rejoice when I saw you turn up at Buschy, but all the same I could not keep away from the hut.

"Perhaps it will cheer you to know that your words, 'Free gift' and 'Finished work' led me at last to see that my years of good works were all for nothing. In leaving the hut one evening, one question was put to me, and I stepped right out into the light, and the revelation I received that night has been my constant theme since . . . I may say your little book, *God's Way of Salvation* is always in a handy pocket, and constantly I find it of great service where too much speaking is inexpedient. JAS. BROWN."

The remaining months of 1918 were spent in Scotland, save for a brief visit to the Annual Missionary Meetings in London. He told the story of what was being done for the soldiers in France, and of how the Lord was prospering the work and giving evidences of His approval in conversions. As few families were not represented by a son or a brother in the scenes of war, his story was listened to with a sympathetic and prayerful interest. War conditions, lighting restrictions, and long hours in factories and workshops were all against special meetings, but in spite of these hindrances fair audiences were got together in Kilbirnie and Motherwell during special efforts in these towns, and a number professed.

The Armistice was signed on Nov. 11th, 1918, and almost immediately large numbers of soldiers were demobilised. Work in the munition factories was suspended, and there was a

General Political Upheaval

in Britain, which made evangelistic efforts very difficult. Notwithstanding these drawbacks, and counting not his years (he was 72 at this time), Mr. Marshall was earnestly engaged. In the spring of 1919 he had special meetings at Ipswich, at Botesdale, at Gislingham, at Cardiff, and at Bath. At all these places there was manifest interest and not a little blessing. At Cardiff a cinema was taken for the Sunday evenings, and was well filled each evening. Although a veteran, the messages from his lips were not lacking in clearness, vigour, and spiritual power.

The month of June saw him engaged in tent work in the East End of Glasgow, along with James A. Anderson. Unfortunately the tent was blown down before the first meeting was held, and for a week until the tent was repaired these two brethren spoke at the street corner. If it was difficult to get the adults, there were plenty of children, and to them the Gospel was preached. A shiny mirror with a Gospel text on the back, a promise that at the end of the address some boy or girl would be the possessor of one, was sufficient to arrest attention; and as the mirror's message was being unfolded while the bairns stood listening, the grown-ups drew near to hear. Thus was the seed sown which was reaped at a later date.

A Visit to Skye

After spending a month in Glasgow, he accompanied Mr. Wm. McKenzie, of Inverness, on a visit to the crofters in ROSS, SKYE, and HARRIS. His story of that tour is best told in his own words.

"We met at Broadford, Skye, on Wednesday, July 2nd, and drove the same evening to Isle Ornsay, nine miles distant. Mr. McKenzie and Mr John Gillies, from Inverness, a native of Skye who speaks Gaelic fluently, had been working in the district several weeks previous to my arrival, and had done a good deal of visiting in the neighbourhood. During my five days' sojourn at this part of Skye we made excursions to surrounding neighbourhoods and distributed quantities of Gospel literature. Through the influence of a friend we were enabled to secure the Established Church for a Sunday evening Gospel service.

"Leaving brother Gillies, who went to visit his relations at Staffin, we took steamer for Kyle of Lochalsh, in Ross-shire, and spent several days in and around the village waiting the arrival of the steamer. Tarbert, Harris, was reached in about six hours. Harris is a bleak and desolate isle, with a population of about five thousand souls. With our supplies of Gospel 'ammunition' we called at the crofters' houses and distributed lots of Gospel literature in Gaelic and English. We were received very cordially, and the books seemed to be much appreciated. We were privileged to have a number of Gospel meetings in the public hall in Tarbert, which is the largest village in the island and the port of call.

"Mr. McKenzie left me at Harris for Inverness, and I went by steamer to Uig, on the north-east of Skye, where there is a considerable crofter settlement. During my week's sojourn at Uig I had innumerable opportunities of personal conversation, and disposed of large quantities of Gospel messages. In addition to this, I had a capital Gospel meeting, which was very well attended.

From Uig I journeyed to Portree, the capital of Skye, which is fifteen miles south of Uig. Although I had not the opportunity of preaching publicly in Portree, I was privileged to pass a number of messages of peace to the visitors and inhabitants in and around the village. Left Portree at 7 a.m. on Saturday, August 2nd, and arrived here *via* Mallaig at 11 p.m. We had hoped to visit North and South Uist, but owing to the limited time at our disposal we were unable to do so. North Uist is largely Protestant, but South Uist and Barra are mostly Roman Catholic.

"The Crofters, generally speaking, are much better off temporally than they were on my first visit to Skye twenty-five years ago. One of the chief hindrances to the spread of the Gospel in the Highlands and Islands is the traditional hyper-calvinistic theology, in which they have been soaked. Many of them hold that God loves the elect alone, that Christ died for some men only, that the faith—necessitating 'irresistible' power of the Holy Spirit—is given to 'His own' alone; and they are strong believers in universal foreordination.

"A fatalistic spell seems to stupify the people, and they say: 'If we are to be saved we will be saved, and if we are to be lost we will be lost!' Not being able to ascertain the fact that God loves them, or that Christ died for them, they wait on the Holy Spirit for a work to be done in them, instead of crediting God's testimony regarding the glorious atonement that was made for them at Calvary.

"A crofter in Skye said to me: 'If I knew that Christ died for me I would be all right.' I asked a bright, intelligent boy the meaning of the word 'world' in John 3:16. Without hesitating he immediately replied, 'All the good people!'"

Revival and Distress

The autumn of 1919 was characterised by considerable activity in Glasgow. Cranston's Picture House, a large palatial building (just opened), in the centre of the City, was secured for Sunday evening services. The response was remarkable, and the building was filled each Sunday long before the advertised hour. Mr. Marshall preached frequently during that winter to the large audiences which gathered during the first, the most truly fruitful, and in every way the best series of Cinema Services held in the City.

After a very active and busy spell, during which missions were held in Liverpool, Birkenhead, Bolton, and Leytonstone, London, he sailed on August 14th, 1920, for the United States, arriving at New York on August 21st. This trip occupied nine months, and it was not until May of the following years that he returned home. During this sojourn in the United States and Canada he travelled from East to West, and visited the scenes of former labours, seeking to establish the saints as well as win souls for Christ.

About this time the distess in Poland, Esthonia, and other countries affected by the Russian Revolution was very acute. The Geneva Red Cross Society and kindred organisations were sending train loads of food and clothing across Europe, but still the cry was for more. Through brethren in the United States and from correspondence with Messrs. Fetler and Podin, of Reval, Mr. Marshall learned of the dire distress and destitution many of the Christians from Soviet Russia were enduring. He did much to stir up action among Christians at home. Food, clothing, boots, and money being forwarded to Reval from Glasgow and Liverpool, largely through his instrumentality.

At the close of the fishing season of 1921 a revival broke out among the Scottish fishermen, then at Yarmouth. On the return of the fleet to Scotland the work spread along the fishing villages of the Moray Firth, and great numbers professed to be saved. This encouraged Mr. Marshall to go to Peterhead, where he was instrumental in establishing the faith of some of the young converts. He was also privileged to see something of the grace of God, and, like Barnabas, he was glad.

Among Old Friends

He ever retained a warm affection for his native

shire and his native town, Stranraer, and endeavoured to spend a little while each year encouraging the saints and strengthening the small Assemblies in the country districts of Wigtownshire. Most of these Assemblies, the fruit of the devoted labours of servants of God now gone to their rest and reward, have suffered through emigration, and the altered conditions of rural life during the past twenty years. His visits were mostly planned to coincide with the tent work in the county, and they were blessed to saint and sinner. In 1923 the visit took place in January, as his plans were made to again visit America in June. He left Glasgow on board the S.S. "Athenia" for his 36th, and what proved to be his last, trip, on June 22, arriving at Montreal on July 2. He remained on the American Continent until April, 1924, spending most of his time among the Assemblies in the province of Ontario. During his stay in Canada he visited Montreal on two occasions, and proved a great help to the Lord's people there. His simple scriptural teaching concerning the work of the Lord Jesus Christ and concerning the unity of all true believers doing much to help them to cast off unscriptural trammels. This last visit and the time spent among brethren beloved, many of them his own children in the faith, was one of the crowning mercies God had reserved for His beloved servant.

He came back to Scotland invigorated and revived with the hope that after a visit to the West Indies in the winter he would again return to old fields and old friends, but God had ordered otherwise.

CHAPTER XII

A Bright Eventide

After his return from America there were indications that the veteran's strength was beginning to wane, and the distressing complaint from which he suffered during the closing years of his life commenced to manifest itself. It was not, however, until the autumn of 1925 that his medical advisers informed him that a considerable hardening of the arteries near the heart had taken place, and that from thenceforth the pace must be slowed and all exertion avoided. A period of complete rest was prescribed, and for three months the energetic veteran bowed to the medical decree, with the result that he benefited so much he was able to take occasional meetings, though he never again undertook a series.

In his comparative retirement, however, his services were turned into other channels. His study at Redcroft became transformed into a little book room, and here he was wont to spend his days. No longer able himself to carry the printed message to the needy, he saw to it that those who would do so were kept supplied. What he aimed at in his writings was circulation, and he was his own best agent in securing this. Carefully selected assortments were made up, and parcelled with his own hands, then despatched with unfailing regularity to isolated or needy workers in Britain, Canada, and the

United States, to be carried by them to croft, hamlet, or shack, or to be placed in the hands of sufferers in hospitals and workhouses. Many a text-carrier bearing aloft his banner with its flaming message was indebted to Mr. Marshall for the supply of Gospel leaflets, which he dealt out as he passed along the causeway.

Joy in Service

His correspondence was conducted with strict punctuality, and letters received from servants of the Lord at home and abroad were preserved to be prayed over first, to be read in the local prayer meeting and to be used in stirring others to greater interest and activity in the Lord's service.

His excursions from home, which were often for a week-end, were a great pleasure to him, and when he was on the platform, like the war horse scenting battle, something of the old fire and the enthusiasm returned. Especially so was this true of his visits to the united services conducted in one of Glasgow's central picture houses on Sunday evenings. With an audience of seven or eight hundred before him, most of them gathered in off the streets, he gave of his best, and presented the Gospel with clearness and great power. A remarkable feature of these week-end meetings was that he rarely preached without seeing some definite result in sinners professing to be saved.

His last meeting which he thus addressed was in Albert Hall, Shawlands, in March, 1928, and he spoke with unction and grip for 45 minutes on his favourite theme. During the after-meeting he was seized with a slight heart attack, from which he quickly recovered, but it then became evident that so far as the platform was concerned the warrior's task was ended.

He still continued his

Ministry of Helping

those active in the fight, but the blood pressure and breathlessness on the slightest exertion made walking and active exercise very difficult. Part of July was spent at Boat-of-Garten, where Mr. and Mrs. Marshall were the guests of their very old friend, Mrs. Gardiner. A season of quiet rest and of peculiar spiritual sweetness, was enjoyed by all in the house during these fourteen days.

He returned to Prestwick before the end of the month benefited by the change, and set to work with all his old vigour. He was able to be at the weekly prayer meeting, where his budget of letters was read and prayed over. On the Lord's Day he was present at the Lord's table, and at the close of the meeting exhorted the saints to greater earnestness in prayer, and greater endeavour in spreading the Gospel. It seemed as the little company dispersed that he endeavoured to get a hand-shake and speak a word of greeting to every person present, while to not a few he handed a small packet of ammunition for distribution during the day.

An Abundant Entrance

An open-air service was held on the beach in the evening at which he was present and took part in prayer. The following day a return of his cough caused him some trouble, but did not interfere with his self-imposed tasks. On Tuesday and Wednesday he made up a great many packets and replied to numerous letters. In the evening of Wednesday, August 8th he complained of being tired. A few hours of restlessness and discomfort, and a short spasm of pain followed, and then the earthly course was ended, and the labourer full of years was at Home with the Lord. His Home-call took place at 1 a.m., on August 9th, 1928.

His Gospel activities only ceased when his life ended, for before the last messages of mercy made up by his own hands, and despatched by post, had reached their destination, the ambassador had been called up higher, and was in the presence of the King.

Thus ended a life lived in the fear of God and in the faith of His Son Jesus Christ; a life of which it could be truly said, it was "life abundant." His was a life peculiarly blessed, in which God fulfilled His promise, "Them that honour Me I will honour" (1 Sam. 2:30). His domestic relationships were happy, and his home was to him a sanctuary. He had great joy in the preaching of the Gospel, and still greater joy in the numerous converts from that preaching. He knew in a way few men have ever learned the blessedness of giving. He was abundantly provided for, and he ended his life in harness as he would have wished to do. Surely an abundant entrance.

He was a man of great transparency of character, in whose heart the love of God had found a large place. His faith was

Simple and Unaffected

Sincere and outspoken, he had all his countrymen's love of a controversy, but never for its own sake. He had the courage to state and to defend what he believed to be right, but he never harboured a grudge and he bore no malice to any man. If men who differed from him abused or maligned him, his answer was: "We must be charitable," or, "God bless them."

He was the most truly "other worldly-minded man" it was ever my privilege to meet. Self-advertisement and self-aggrandisement made no appeal to his nature. His greatest pleasure in life was to give. No one who performed the smallest service for him was forgotten, and wherever he could, he gave of that which God had entrusted him without thought of recompense or reward.

Frequently friends heard him speak of the Lord's account, but few if any knew what that meant. From the day of his conversion he honoured the Lord with his substance, and gave systematically as the Lord had prospered him. In early life he commenced to give a twelfth to the Lord of all he received, and this was gradually increased until for years before his death he set aside an eighth of his total income to be used in the Lord's service.

Universally

Loved and Trusted

he was the steward of no inconsiderable sum, but his diaries show this was faithfully recorded and conscientiously dealt with as before God. Few works of faith and labours of love known to him were overlooked. Lonely workers in the homeland and Canada can tell that Mr. Marshall's letter of cheer also brought with it a token of practical fellowship. In this way he must have been a succourer of many. It is not given to all to give as he gave. Indeed, but for a great measure of self-denial on the part of husband and wife, it would not have been possible for Mr. Marshall to distribute so freely as he did, but his simplicity and devotedness in this as in other matters should be a rebuke to the pride and worldliness to which most of us must plead guilty. His example and abundant entrance should encourage others to follow his faith.

His remains were committed to their resting place in Prestwick Cemetery, on August 11th, amid a storm of wind and rain, but accompanied by the mingled mourning and praise of nearly three hundred brethren, many of whom were led to Christ through his instrumentality. Brief services were held in the home and at Bute Hall, at which Wm. Hamilton, W.J. Grant, R.W. Smith, John Gray, and John Hawthorn took part. Mr. Smith and Mr. Gray conducted the service in the Cemetery.

A simple stone marks the hallowed spot where, facing the sunrise, the Lord's "redeemed one" lies, waiting the moment of resurrection and reunion, and underneath the modest particular of his name and age, there is inscribed thereon in indestructible letters his favourite text: "For God so loved the world, that He gave His only begotten Son, that whosoever believeth in him should not perish, but have everlasting life" (John 3:16).

Mrs. Marshall survived her husband for another twenty years when "Redcroft", which had been their home for almost half a century, was left as a home for missionaries on furlough. For more than thirty years it served that purpose and during that time many of the Lord's servants had happy furloughs there, just a few yards from Prestwick beach. When at last the reduced number of missionaries and the different pattern of furloughs rendered it no longer necessary, it was sold and the proceeds from it are still being used for the benefit of the Lord's servants.

And sixty years after its erection, Alexander Marshall's gravestone in Prestwick cemetery still boldly proclaims that, "God so loved the world that He gave His only begotten Son."

A Year in the Life of Alexander Marshall

The following information has been culled from *The Believers' Magazine* for 1891, the first year of publication of the magazine.

The January issue mentioned that Mr. Marshall had recently returned from Canada and had been conducting meetings in Hamilton, Lanarkshire. The Town Hall was well filled on Sunday nights and sinners had been converted. Later news mentioned in the same issue said that the meetings continued to be well attended.

The same issue reported that Mr. Marshall had had meetings in Grosvenor Hall, Rathgar, Ireland. It wasn't clear whether these gospel meetings preceded or followed those in Hamilton. Both series must have taken place towards the end of 1890 as the next item shows.

Mr. Marshall and Dr. Norman Case from Canada were among the speakers at the Aberdeen New Year conference and they stayed on for a gospel campaign. The Alhambra Hall, holding 1,500, was crowded on Sunday evenings and souls had been saved. The March issue of the magazine said that the meetings continued to be well attended till the last. The weeknight meetings were conducted in the George Street Hall and not a few were born again. In April the magazine reported that the Sunday evening meetings in the Alhambra had been concluded, the closing meetings having been conducted by Dr. Case, John Ritchie and John McGaw of Aberdeen.

The same issue of the magazine said that Mr. Marshall had had a fortnight's meetings in the Lesser Town Hall in Cumnock. The meetings were fairly well attended and several professed conversion. (The Cumnock assembly must have died out later since it was re-established after a campaign by Joseph Strain.)

From Cumnock the Lord's servant proceeded to Carlisle where he had two weeks' meetings in The City Hall. Attendance was good and there was fruit in conversions.

The next issue, May's, showed that Mr. Marshall was back in Ayrshire, at Galston where he had three weeks' meetings. The meetings were large and there was a number of clear cases of conversion.

In mid May the Lord's servant joined Henry Dyer, W.H. Hunter of Manchester, W.H. Bennett, W. Macdonald of Penang, W. Maclean of Belfast, John Ritchie, W. McLaughland of Belfast, W. Laing, and A.J. Holiday at a conference in Bradford, Yorkshire. (Mr. Dyer was called home on July 2.)

He is next found in Ayrshire again, this time in a tent at Girvan in June working with Arthur Hodgkinson, who had been saved under his preaching in Rugby, Ontario. This was not the Ayrshire Tent, as it was pitched at the same time in the town of Ayr where the preacher was W. Montgomerie.

At the end of the same month the evangelist was in Dumfries with a tent in the Dock Park, and Robert Gall of Carlisle was his partner. (The same issue reported that Messrs. Hodgkinson and Gall had pitched a tent in Kirkcudbright.) The next issue indicates that Wm. Maclean of Belfast was with Mr. Marshall in the tent in Dumfries and that blessing had been experienced. In fact Mr. Marshall reported, "We have decided to remain here till the close of the tent season. Meetings are larger, and a number of clear cases of conversion." The October magazine said that the tent had been taken down and the meetings transferred to a hall, where the assembly had commenced to meet a few months before.

Mr. Marshall was at a conference in Grangemouth in early October where his fellow preachers were

J.H. Burridge and John Ritchie. Arther Hodgkinson was helping the young believers in Dumfries and preaching the gospel in the new hall in the town. Meantime Mr. Marshall had again been in Ireland, at Cork where a new hall had just been opened.

The final magazine of the year reported the renting of Abingdon Hall, Partick as the meeting-place of an assembly and Alex Marshall was conducting a campaign with considerable interest and blessing among the unsaved.

Places Visited by A. Marshall

A
Albany, Jamaica 82
Alexandria 74
Ayr 64

B
Barbados 84
Barrow 64
Bath 134
Belleville, Ontario 50
Birkenhead 137
Blackburn 64
Blackrock, U.S.A. 46
Bolton 150
Bristol 64
British Guiana 81, 85, 87, 94, 95
Buffalo 46

C
Cairo 74
California 68
Cardiff 64
Carlisle 64
Carthagena, Colombia 84
Chicago 71
Colombia 75
Colon, Colombia 75, 83

D
Detroit 71, 96
Dumfries 62

E
Egypt 74

G
Georgetown, Guyana 87
Glasgow 64, 134, 137, 141, 142
Greytown, Nicaragua 75
Guelph 50

H
Hamilton, Ontario 46
Harris 135
Harrisburg, U.S.A. 46
Harrogate 64
Henrietta, West Indies 86
Hobart 47
Holland 129

I
Iceland 72
Ipswich 134

J
Jamaica 82, 83

K
Kilmarnock 61, 62
Kingston, Jamaica 82, 83
Kyle of Lochalsh 135

L
Leeds 63
Liverpool 137
London 133, 137

M
Manchester 62, 63, 64

150

Mexico 75, 83
Montreal 139

N
New Hebrides 76
New Westminster, Canada 60
New York 71
New Zealand 168, 176
Nicaragua 75
Norwich 64

O
Ontario 99, 100, 139
Orillia, Canada 46, 47, 51, 53, 54, 60, 92

P
Palestine 74
Panama 83
Peterhead 138
Pickersgill, Canada 85
Pittsburg 46
Pomeroon, Guiana 85
Port Antonio, Jamaica 83
Portland 60
Port of Spain, Trinidad 84
Portree 136
Prestwick 68
Pyramids 74

R
Reykjavik 73
Ross-shire 135
Rouen 132

Rugby 50
Russia 87

S
San Francisco 56
Santa Cruz 75
St. Catherines 46
St. Louis 46
St. Petersburg 88, 89
St. Thomas 75
Seattle 60
Selkirk 55
Seven Bridge, Canada 47
Siglafjord 73
Skye 135
Stranraer 139

T
Toronto 42, 49, 54
Trinidad 84

U
Uig 136
U.S.A. 130, 137

V
Vancouver 56, 60, 92
Vera Cruz 60
Victoria, Canada 60

W
Wales 78
Warminster 44
West Indies 81, 94, 130
Winnipeg 55

Friends and Colleagues
of A. Marshall

A
Aitchison, C. 63
Anderson, Jas. A. 134
Andrews, Mrs. 50
Ashlyn, Quinton 80

B
Baedeker, Dr. 91
Benner, G. 51
Benner, S.W. 51, 54, 92
Bird, Cyril 50
Brown, Jas. 133
Byrnell, Mr. 130, 132

C
Caldwell, J.R. 32, 33, 34, 36, 67
Campbell, Jas. 41
Carnie, J.M. 41
Chapman, R.C. 39
Curtis, Mr. and Mrs. 84

D
Dunn, W.D. 33

F
Fetler, Mr. 89, 138
Finlay, D.J. 33, 39
Forlong, G. 19, 76

G
Gallop, Miss 84
Gardiner, Mrs. 142

G (cont.)
Gillies, John 135
Glenarthur, Lord 24
Goodfellow, J. 56, 57
Gook, A. 72
Grant, W.J. 145
Gray, J. 145
Grenfell, D. 73
Grove, Geo. 50

H
Haines, Mr. 49
Hambleton, John 38
Hodgkinson, A.E. 50

I
Irving, Rick 46, 49

J
Johnstone, Rose 82

K
Kargel, Mr. 91
Kirk, Dr. 30

L
Lieven, Princess 88
Lincoln, W. 39
Lockett, Mr. 50

Mc
McKenzie, W. 135, 136
McVicker, J.G. 38, 49

M
Maury, Mr. 82
Moody, D.L. 32
Moorhouse, Hy. 38
Morison, Jas. 14, 30, 32
Morley, John 38
Morton, Chas. 39, 63
Munro, Donald 39, 41

N
Nichols, W.W. 85, 86

O
Ord, Harrison 39
Orton, J.A. 51
Osborne, Todd 31
Owens, R.W. 41

P
Pickering, Hy. 113
Prokhanoff, Ivan 88

Q
Quarrier, W. 33

R
Rea, D. 64, 120

Rea, T. 120
Roberts, Evan 78, 79
Robertson, D. 72
Ross, Donald 38, 41, 42, 45,
56, 66

S
Sankey, I.D. 32
Smith, C.G. 86
Smith, John 39, 41, 45
Sparrow, Mr. and Mrs. 84,
86
Stewart, A. 33, 36, 124
Strong, Leon. 81, 95
Swift, Mrs. 95

T
Tate, Amy 49
Todd, Alice 31

V
Varley, Hy. 40

W
Wales, Mr. 87
Watson, C.P. 120